FRUIT
OF THE SPIRIT

DEEPENING
LIFE
TOGETHER

FRUIT
OF THE SPIRIT

LifeTogether

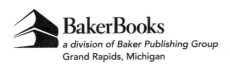

BakerBooks
a division of Baker Publishing Group
Grand Rapids, Michigan

© 2011 by Lifetogether Publishing

Published by Baker Books
a division of Baker Publishing Group
P.O. Box 6287, Grand Rapids, MI 49516-6287
www.bakerbooks.com

Printed in the United States of America

Library of Congress Cataloging-in-Publication Data
Fruit of the spirit.
    p. cm. — Deepening life together)
    Includes bibliographical references.
    ISBN 978-0-8010-6936-9 (pbk.)
    1. Fruit of the Spirit—Study and teaching. 2. Christian life—Study and teaching.
BV4511.F77 2011
234′.13—dc22   2011005617

11 12 13 14 15 16 17   7 6 5 4 3 2 1

green press INITIATIVE

CONTENTS

Contents

ACKNOWLEDGMENTS

The *Deepening Life Together: Fruit of the Spirit* Small Group Video Bible Study has come together through the efforts of many at Baker Publishing Group, Lifetogether Publishing, and Lamplighter Media for which we express our heartfelt thanks.

Executive Producer	John Nill
Producer and Director	Sue Doc Ross
Editors	Mark L. Strauss (Scholar), Teresa Haymaker
Curriculum Development	Brett Eastman, Sue Doc Ross, Mark L. Strauss, Teresa Haymaker, Stephanie French
Video Production	Chris Balish, Rodney Bissell, Nick Calabrese, Sebastian Hoppe Fuentes, Josh Greene, Patrick Griffin, Teresa Haymaker, Oziel Jabin Ibarra, Natali Ibarra, Janae Janik, Keith Sorrell, Lance Tracy, Sophie Olson, Ian Ross
Teachers and Scholars	Tim Theule, Lynn Cohick, Erik Thoennes, Mark Strauss, Craig Keener, Joanne Jung
Baker Publishing Group	Jack Kuhatschek

Special thanks to: DeLisa Ivy, Bethel Seminary, Talbot School of Theology, Wheaton College

Clips from The JESUS Film are copyright © 1995–2010 The JESUS Film Project®. A ministry of Campus Crusade for Christ International®.

Interior icons by Tom Clark

READ ME FIRST

Welcome to the *Deepening Life Together* study on *Fruit of the Spirit*. For some of you, this might be the first time you've connected in a small group community. We want you to know that God cares about you and your spiritual growth. As you prayerfully respond to the principles you learn in this study, God will move you to a deeper level of commitment and intimacy with himself, as well as with those in your small group.

We at Baker Books and Lifetogether Publishing look forward to hearing the stories of how God changes you from the inside out during this small group experience. We pray God blesses you with all he has planned for you through this journey together.

> For the LORD is good and his love endures forever;
> his faithfulness continues through all generations.
>
> Psalm 100:5

Session Outline

Most people want to live a healthy, balanced spiritual life, but few achieve this by themselves. And most small groups struggle to balance all of God's purposes in their meetings. Groups tend to overemphasize one of the five purposes, perhaps fellowship or discipleship.

Rarely is there a healthy balance that includes evangelism, ministry, and worship. That's why we've included all of these elements in this study so you can live a healthy, balanced spiritual life over time.

A typical group session will include the following:

Memory Verses

For each session we have provided a Memory Verse that emphasizes an important truth from the session. This is an optional exercise, but we believe that memorizing Scripture can be a vital part of filling our minds with God's Word. We encourage you to give this important habit a try.

CONNECTING *with God's Family (Fellowship)*

The foundation for spiritual growth is an intimate connection with God and his family. A few people who really know you and who earn your trust provide a place to experience the life Jesus invites you to live. This section of each session typically offers you two activities.

You can get to know your whole group by using the icebreaker question, and/or you can check in with one or two group members— your spiritual partner(s)—for a deeper connection and encouragement in your spiritual journey.

DVD Teaching Segment

A *Deepening Life Together: Fruit of the Spirit* Video Teaching DVD companion to this study guide is available. For each study session, the DVD contains a lesson taught by Tim Theule. If you are using the DVD, you will view the teaching segment after your *Connecting* discussion and before your group discussion time (the *Growing* section).

GROWING *to Be Like Christ (Discipleship)*

Here is where you come face-to-face with Scripture. In core passages you'll explore what the Bible teaches about the topic of the study.

The focus won't be on accumulating information but on how we should live in light of the Word of God. We want to help you apply the Scriptures practically, creatively, and from your heart as well as your head. At the end of the day, allowing the timeless truths from God's Word to transform our lives in Christ is our greatest aim.

DEVELOPING *Your Gifts to Serve Others (Ministry)*

Jesus trained his disciples to discover and develop their gifts to serve others. And God has designed each of us uniquely to serve him in a way no other person can. This section will help you discover and use your God-given design. It will also encourage your group to discover your unique design as a community. In this study, you'll put into practice what you've learned in the Bible study by taking a step to serve others. These simple steps will take your group on a faith journey that could change your lives forever.

SHARING *Your Life Mission Every Day (Evangelism)*

Many people skip over this aspect of the Christian life because it's scary, relationally awkward, or simply too much work for their busy schedules. But Jesus wanted all of his disciples to help outsiders connect with him, to know him personally. This doesn't mean preaching on street corners. It could mean welcoming a few newcomers into your group, hosting a short-term group in your home, or walking through this study with a friend. In this study, you'll have an opportunity to go beyond Bible study to biblical living.

SURRENDERING *Your Life for God's Pleasure (Worship)*

God is most pleased by a heart that is fully his. Each group session will give you a chance to surrender your heart to God in prayer and worship. You may read a psalm together, share a page in your journal, or sing a song to close your meeting. If you have never prayed aloud in a group before, no one will pressure you. Instead, you'll experience the support of others who are praying for you.

Study Notes

This section provides background notes on the Bible passage(s) you examine in the *Growing* section. You may want to refer to these notes during your group meeting or as a reference for those doing additional study.

For Deeper Study (optional)

Some sessions provide *For Deeper Study*. If you want to dig deeper into more Bible passages about the topic at hand, we've provided additional passages and questions. Your group may choose to do study homework ahead of each meeting in order to cover more biblical material. Or you as an individual may choose to study the *For Deeper Study* on your own. If you prefer not to do study homework, the *Growing* section will provide you with plenty to discuss within the group. These options allow individuals or the whole group to go deeper in their study, while still accommodating those who can't do homework or are new to your group. You can record your discoveries in your journal. We encourage you to read some of your insights to a friend (spiritual partner) for accountability and support. Spiritual partners may check in each week over the phone, through e-mail, or at the beginning of the group meeting.

Reflections

On the *Reflections* pages we provide Scriptures to read and reflect on between group meetings. We suggest you use this section to seek God at home throughout the week. This time at home should begin and end with prayer. Don't get in a hurry; take enough time to hear God's direction.

Subgroup for Discussion and Prayer

If your group is large (more than seven people), we encourage you to separate into groups of two to four for discussion and prayer. This is to encourage greater participation and deeper discussion.

INTRODUCTION

Stories containing word pictures have been used throughout history to capture the imagination, bring ideas to life, invite contemplation and reflection, and challenge thought. One such story is the tale of the storyteller, Scheherazade, whose fables have been preserved in a work known as the *Arabian Nights*. The story of Scheherazade goes like this:

Shahryar, king of Persia, upon discovering his wife's infidelity, has her executed and declares all women to be unfaithful. He then begins to marry a succession of virgins, only to execute each one the next morning. Eventually there are no more virgins to be found in the kingdom. With one exception. The daughter of the king's political advisor, whose job it is to find virgins for the king to marry. Over the protests of her father, Scheherazade offers herself as the king's next bride.

On the night of their wedding, Scheherazade begins to tell the king a story, but leaves the tale hanging, saying she will finish it the next night. The king really wants to hear the end of the story, so he is forced to postpone her execution in order to hear the ending. The next night, as soon as Scheherazade finishes the story, she begins a new one. Again, she leaves the story hanging, hoping to buy herself another day of life. The king, eager to hear the conclusion, postpones her execution once again. As the story goes, this continues for 1,001 nights.

The apostle Paul used word pictures in his epistles to help his hearers, and us, understand the things of God. The *fruit of the Spirit* in Galatians 5:22–23 is one such word picture in Scripture designed to make us think. While Scheherazade told stories to save herself, Paul and the other writers of the Scriptures use word pictures to save others. They accomplish this by leading their readers to the knowledge of their Lord and Savior, Jesus Christ. Over the next six sessions, we will examine the meaning of the fruit in Paul's word picture in Galatians 5:22–23 together.

GOD'S PURPOSE FOR YOU

MEMORY VERSE: But the fruit of the Spirit is love, joy, peace, patience, kindness, goodness, faithfulness, gentleness and self-control. Against such things there is no law (Gal. 5:22–23).

James loves to garden using a mix of colors and textures to bring out the natural beauty of the plants and landscape. One of his favorite things is tending to the many fruit trees he has planted around his property. Fruit trees provide beauty, shade, and the added benefit of great-tasting fruit, but growing them is not an easy task. They require a lot of tending. Even before he planted them, he had to consider location, soil, drainage, spacing between trees, and pollination requirements. Then, once his trees were planted and growing, they continuously needed water, fertilizer, pruning, and protection against fungal and insect problems. It takes devotion to grow fruit trees, but with proper care and feeding they can live a long time and be very productive.

James has a small collection of recently planted fruit trees that haven't yet produced any fruit, but he's anticipating it. He's looking forward to getting apples from the apple trees, pears from the pear trees, and cherries from the cherry trees. Each tree will produce fruit in keeping with its kind as designed by God.

In Galatians 5:22–23, the apostle Paul gives us a great word picture to illustrate what the fruit of God's Spirit will become once they mature. This is a powerful word picture loaded with meaning. In this session we will begin to unpack that meaning as we grow in understanding of God's plan and purpose for the fruit of the Spirit in our lives.

 ## CONNECTING

10 min.

Begin your group time with prayer. Ask God for open minds and willing hearts to receive his Word through this Bible study and for the courage to change as he challenges you in the weeks to come.

Deeper relationships happen when we take time to keep in touch with one another. As you begin, pass around a copy of the *Small Group Roster*, a sheet of paper, or one of your study guides, opened to the *Small Group Roster*. When the roster gets to you, write down your contact information, including the best time and method for contacting you. Then, someone volunteer to make copies or type up a list with everyone's information and e-mail it to the group this week.

1. Begin this first session by introducing yourselves. Include your name, what you do for a living, what you do for fun, and anything else you would like to share.

2. Whether your group is new or ongoing, it's always important to reflect on and review your group values. In the *Appendix* is a *Small Group Agreement* with values most useful in sustaining healthy, balanced groups. Review these values and choose one or two—values you haven't previously focused on or have room to grow in—to emphasize during this study. Choose those that will take your group to the next stage of intimacy and spiritual health. Discuss how you will implement these values in your small group.

3. What about gardening do you find gratifying or satisfying?

GROWING

45–50 min.

From the first page of the Bible we discover that God creates a world that is not stagnant but full of life. It is by his design and for his purposes that humanity was created and given everything needed to grow into people of God.

God Created Humankind and Placed Them in a Garden
Read Genesis 2:8–17.

4. What was humanity's first home like?

   Why do you think God made humanity's home where he did?

5. What is the purpose of the plant life and other things God placed in the garden?

6. Why do you think God placed a tree in the garden that was off limits (see the *Study Notes* for insight)?

7. What does this passage say about why God created us (v. 15)?

We Were Created for Growth
Read Colossians 1:9–11.

8. What are five purposes that God fulfills in our lives as we grow in spiritual wisdom and understanding (vv. 10–11)?

9. How do these purposes represent growth in our Christian lives?

   What is God's part in this?

Read 1 Corinthians 3:5–11.

10. What is the seed that Paul refers to in verse 6?

11. What does this verse say about our responsibility as God's children?

12. What is our purpose in God's plan?

Recipients of the Spirit of God

Read Ephesians 1:13–14.

13. What is the role of the Spirit in our lives, according to this passage?

14. What does it mean to be included "in Christ"?

   How do we become included "in Christ"?

Read 1 John 4:13–16.

15. How do you think we can know that we have the Spirit of God within us?

16. What is the ultimate purpose of our salvation and indwelling of the Holy Spirit in us, according to verse 15?

Fruitfulness Is God's Purpose for Us

From the beginning of time, God's purpose and plan for humanity has been to be fruitful and multiply (Gen. 1:28). Just like we want our garden to produce fruit (fruits, vegetables, foliage, or flowers), God desires that his garden produces fruit—fruit that is the result of our growth in these character qualities: love, joy, peace, patience, kindness, goodness, faithfulness, gentleness, and self-control. God has given us the Spirit to make this happen. God is the master gardener for our growth; he is not finished with us. He loves us as we are, but he's intent on growing us into the people he desires us to be—people of character, people like Jesus.

17. What character-building fruit have you experienced in your life lately?

DEVELOPING

10 min.

Developing our ability to serve God as the Holy Spirit leads requires that we make time to let God speak to us daily.

18. Which of the following next steps toward this goal are you willing to take for the next few weeks?

☐ *Prayer.* Commit to connecting with God daily through personal prayer. It's important to separate yourself from the distractions in your life so you can really focus on communicating with God. Some people find it helpful to write out their prayers in a journal.

☐ *Reflection.* At the end of each session you'll find *Reflections* Scriptures that specifically relate to the topic of our study for the session. These are provided to give you an opportunity for reading a short Bible passage five days a week during the course of this study. Write down your insights on what you read each day in the space provided. On the sixth day, summarize what God has shown you throughout the week.

☐ *Meditation.* Psalm 119:11 says: "I have hidden your word in my heart that I might not sin against you." Meditation is focused attention on the Word of God and is a great way to internalize God's Word more deeply. One way to do this is to write a portion of Scripture on a card and tape it somewhere where you're sure to see it often, such as your bathroom mirror, car's dashboard, or the kitchen table. Think about it as you get dressed in the morning, when you sit at red lights, or while you're eating a meal. Reflect on what God is saying to you through his words. Consider using the passages provided in the *Reflections* pages in each session. As you meditate upon these Scriptures, you will notice them beginning to take up residence in your heart and mind.

SHARING

10 min.

Jesus lived and died so that humankind might come to know him and be reconciled to God through him. The Holy Spirit empowers

19

us to live out God's purposes for us. One of these purposes is to be his witnesses to the people around us.

19. Jesus wants all of his disciples to help others connect with him, to know him personally. In the weeks to come, you'll be asked to identify and share with people in your circle of influence who need to know Jesus or need to connect with him through a small group community. With this in mind, as you go about your day-to-day activities this week, pay special attention to the people God has placed in your life. There may be co-workers, family or friends, other parents at school or sporting events that you see or talk to on a regular basis. When we meet next time, we'll talk about how to help connect believers to Christian community and begin sharing Jesus with those who don't yet know him.

SURRENDERING

10 min.

Jeremiah 29:13 says, "You will seek me and find me when you seek me with all your heart." God promises to be there for us when we yield our hearts fully to him. Each week you will have a chance to surrender your hearts to God in worship and prayer.

20. Consider some different ways to worship that might fit your group. Following are a few ideas. Spend a few minutes worshiping God together.

☐ Have someone use their musical gifts to lead the group in a worship song. You might sing a simple chorus a cappella, with guitar/piano accompaniment, or with a worship CD.

☐ Read a passage of Scripture aloud together, making it a time of praise and worship as the words remind you of all God has done for you. Choose a psalm or other favorite verses.

☐ Spend a few minutes praising God aloud. You may highlight some of the attributes of God's character or praise him for specific circumstances in your life.

21. Every believer should have a plan for spending time alone with God. Your time with God is personal and reflects who you are in relationship with him. However you choose to spend your time with him, try to allow time for praise, prayer, and reading of Scripture. *Reflections* are provided at the end of each session for you to use as part of your daily time with God. These will offer reinforcement of the principles you are learning, and develop or strengthen your habit of time alone with God throughout the week.

22. Before you close your group in prayer, answer this question: "How can we pray for you this week?" Write prayer requests on your *Prayer and Praise Report* and commit to praying for each other throughout the week. Close in prayer, asking God to encourage each participant to embrace the fruit of the Spirit and begin to live them out daily.

Study Notes

Tree of the knowledge of good and evil: This tree signifies the giving of knowledge of good and evil. In contrast to the tree of life, eating of this tree would ultimately lead to death. The knowledge referred to is moral knowledge (discernment). Since God created Adam and Eve, they already possessed the moral discernment given them from God. In eating from the tree, they were disobeying God and therefore gained an understanding of evil, which is disobedience. If Adam had not disobeyed God, he would never have come to know evil. It was not therefore a "power" imbued by the tree that gave this knowledge but the act of disobedience in eating from it.

For Deeper Study (Optional)

Read Psalm 92:12–14 below. Pay close attention to the italicized phrases.

On a sheet of paper or in your journal, note what these passages say (just the facts), what they mean (what can be implied from the text), and what they might mean to you. Once you have completed this for each passage, identify what you think the point is of Psalm 92:12–14.

¹²*The righteous will flourish* like a palm tree, they will grow like a cedar of Lebanon;

¹³*planted in the house of the Lord*, they will flourish in the courts of our God.

¹⁴*They will still bear fruit in old age*, they will stay fresh and green.

Reflections

Reading, reflecting, and meditating on the Word of God is essential to getting to know him deeply. As you read the verses each day, give prayerful consideration to what you learn about God, his Spirit, and his place in your life. Then record your thoughts, insights, or prayer in the *Reflect* section below the verses you read. On the sixth day, record a summary of what you learned over the entire week through this study.

Day 1. Trust in the LORD with all your heart and lean not on your own understanding; in all your ways acknowledge him, and he will make your paths straight (Prov. 3:5–6).

REFLECT

_____

_____

_____

_____

Day 2. Remain in me, and I will remain in you. No branch can bear fruit by itself; it must remain in the vine. Neither can you bear fruit unless you remain in me (John 15:4).

REFLECT

_____

_____

_____

_____

Day 3. For this very reason, make every effort to add to your faith goodness; and to goodness, knowledge; and to knowledge, self-control; and to self-control, perseverance; and to perseverance, godliness; and to godliness, brotherly kindness; and to brotherly kindness, love (2 Peter 1:5–7).

REFLECT

_____

_____

_____

_____

Day 4. For if you possess these qualities in increasing measure, they will keep you from being ineffective and unproductive in your knowledge of our Lord Jesus Christ (2 Peter 1:8).

REFLECT

_____

_____

_____

_____

Day 5. With this in mind, we constantly pray for you, that our God may count you worthy of his calling, and that by his power he may fulfill every good purpose of yours and every act prompted by your faith (2 Thess. 1:11).

REFLECT

_____

_____

_____

_____

Day 6. Use the following space to write any insight God has put in your heart and mind about the things we have looked at in this session and during your _Reflections_ time this week.

SUMMARY

_____

_____

_____

_____

ATTACK OF THE FLESH

MEMORY VERSE: So I say, live by the Spirit, and you will not gratify the desires of the sinful nature (Gal. 5:16).

Tia's boyfriend was a drug dealer, selling stimulants, depressants, and marijuana to his wide network of friends. Neither Tia nor her boyfriend were heavy users of the drugs, but Tia's sister, Marie, was a drug addict in the worst way.

One rainy night in 1969, Marie and her boyfriend were looking to get high, but their drug of choice, heroin, was not available to them until morning. They asked Tia to get them something to get them through the night. For Marie, this was a fatal choice. For the rest of them, it led to a period of mourning and being haunted by guilt for their part in Marie's death.

What makes a person turn to drugs? Common sense and logic tell us drugs only lead to dark and fruitless lives. But people get swept into the life anyway. And there are many complex reasons that all culminate in one thing—humanity's sinful nature.

The Bible tells us we were created for something better—God's eternal love. When we accept God's free gift of salvation through faith in Jesus Christ, we are planted with the Holy Spirit to grow and be fruitful. But in our sinful nature, there are things that can inhibit, thwart, and destroy fruitfulness in our lives. These things are referred to as things of "the flesh."

CONNECTING   *10 min.*

Open your group with prayer. Invite the Holy Spirit to remove any uncertainty that you may have in the power of God to transform your heart.

1. If you have new people joining you for the first time, take a few minutes to briefly introduce yourselves.

2. Share a time when you really wanted something but forces in your life prevented you from having your way. How did things turn out?

GROWING   *45–50 min.*

Flesh is defined as that sinful, selfish part of us that seeks a life apart from God, for ourselves, independent of faith. In this session we will discover how to identify the sins of the flesh and fight against them.

Facing the Sinful Nature (Flesh)
Read Galatians 5:16–21.

3. What do you think it means to live, or walk, by the Spirit?

4. In order to face the sinful nature (flesh), we must know what the sinful nature is. How does verse 17 describe the sinful nature? To what does the "sinful nature," or "flesh," refer?

5. How does verse 17 explain our need for a life that is controlled by the Holy Spirit?

6. What do you think Paul means in verse 19 when he says that the sins of the sinful nature (flesh) are "obvious"?

7. Paul enumerates 15 vices that stem from following our sinful nature. What does the sinful nature (flesh) as described in this passage look like in a person's life (vv. 19–21)?

8. Sins of self-indulgence are what most people think of when they think of the sinful nature (flesh). What are the sins of self-indulgence found in verses 19–21?

9. Sins of self-righteousness are relational sins that often arise when we think we're right and others around us are wrong. What are the sins of self-righteousness in verses 19–21?

10. Paul's letter to the Galatians was written to churches that were struggling with false teaching that claimed that salvation came not by faith alone but by faith plus keeping the Old Testament law. What do we learn from the fact that even very religious people can still be living apart from God?

Fighting the Sinful Nature (Flesh)

11. Romans 13:14 says, "Rather, clothe yourselves with the Lord Jesus Christ, and do not think about how to gratify the desires of the sinful nature." What must we do to fight the enemy of fruitfulness—the sinful nature (flesh)?

Read Galatians 5:24–6:10.

12. What happens to the sinful nature once we belong to Christ, according to verse 5:24?

13. Is there something the believer must do to keep the sinful nature from enveloping our lives (vv. 5:24–6:10)?

In our perpetual fight against home and garden pests, we must face the fact that we'll never eliminate them all permanently. We've got to keep up the fight. It's a continual battle. But we can, through vigilance and ongoing action, limit their impact. The same is true for facing and fighting our flesh. On this side of heaven, our lives will never be flesh-free, but by fighting through faith in Christ and the gospel, we can limit and neutralize the impact of our flesh in our lives so that we can still be fruitful. It's not easy, to be sure, but it's so worth it.

DEVELOPING   *10 min.*

Accountability means being answerable to another for our actions. Spiritual accountability happens when we invite someone into our life for the purpose of encouraging our faith journey and challenging us in specific areas of desired growth. Hebrews 3:12–13 says: "See to it, brothers, that none of you has a sinful, unbelieving heart that turns away from the living God. But encourage one another daily, as long as it is called Today, so that none of you may be hardened by sin's deceitfulness." Opening our lives to someone and making ourselves vulnerable to their loving admonition could perhaps be one of the most difficult things to do; however, it could also result in the deepest and most lasting spiritual growth we've known.

14. Scripture tells us in Ephesians 4:25, "laying aside falsehood, speak truth each one of you with his neighbor, for we are members of one another" (NASB). With this in mind, take a moment to pair up with someone in your group to be your spiritual partner for the remainder of this study. We strongly recommend men partner with men, and women with women. (Refer to the *Leader's Notes* for this question in the *Appendix* for information on what it means to be a spiritual partner.)

    Turn to the *Personal Health Plan* in the *Appendix*. In the box that says "WHO are you connecting with spiritually?" write your partner's name.

    In the box that says "WHAT is your next step for growth?" write one step you would like to take for growth during this study. Tell your partner what step you chose. When you check in with your partner each meeting, the "Partner's Progress" column on this chart will provide a place to record your partner's progress in the goal he or she chose.

15. Spending time together outside of group meetings helps to build stronger relationships within your group as you get to know each other better. Discuss whether your group would like to have a potluck or other type of social to celebrate together what God is doing in your group. You could plan to share a meal prior to a group meeting or plan to follow your completion of this study with a meal together—maybe a barbecue. Appoint one or two people who can follow up with everyone outside of group time to put a plan together.

SHARING

10 min.

The people in your life with whom you come into regular contact make up your circles of influence or *Circles of Life.*

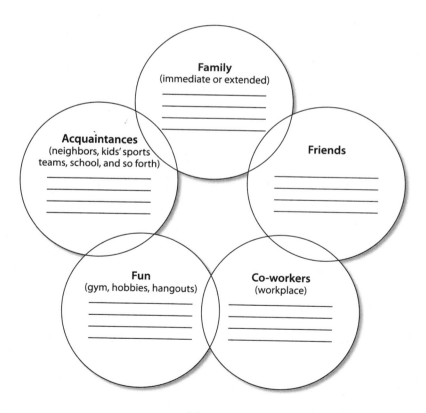

29

16. Take a look at the *Circles of Life* diagram above and think of people you know in each category who need to be connected in Christian community. Write the names of two or three people in each circle.

   The people who fill these circles are not there by accident. God has strategically placed each of them within your sphere of influence because he has equipped you to minister to them and share with them in ways no one else can. Consider the following ideas for reaching out to one or two of the people you listed and make a plan to follow through with them this week.

   ☐ This is a wonderful time to welcome a few friends into your group. Which of the people you listed could you invite? It's possible that you may need to help your friend overcome obstacles to coming to a place where he or she can encounter Jesus. Does your friend need a ride to the group or help with child care?

   ☐ Consider inviting a friend to attend a weekend church service with you and possibly plan to enjoy a meal together afterward. This can be a great opportunity to talk with someone about your faith in Jesus.

   ☐ Is there someone who is unable to attend your group or church but who still needs a connection? Would you be willing to have lunch or coffee with that person, catch up on life, and share something you've learned from this study? Jesus doesn't call all of us to lead small groups, but he does call every disciple to spiritually multiply his or her life over time.

 SURRENDERING   *10 min.*

Deuteronomy 32:3–4 declares: "I will proclaim the name of the LORD. Oh, praise the greatness of our God! He is the Rock, his works are perfect, and all his ways are just." Only our perfect God is worthy of praise.

17. Focus on the words of David as you read Psalm 145 aloud together in an attitude of corporate worship.

18. Take a few minutes to talk about what it would take to make time with God a priority every day or even five or six days a week. Don't put time demands on yourself at first; just make it a priority to draw near to God for a few minutes each day, and gradually you will desire more. Use the *Reflections* at the end of each session as a starting point.

19. Share your prayer requests as a group. Be sure to record everyone's requests on your *Prayer and Praise Report*. Use these as reminders to pray for everyone throughout the week.

    After sharing, gather in smaller circles of three or four people to pray for one another. Be careful not to pressure anyone who may not be comfortable praying aloud. When you pray for each person, you may find it meaningful to hold hands or place your hands on each other's shoulders. Jesus often touched people to communicate his care for them.

Study Notes

Walk: *Walk* is used in the Bible to refer to one's pattern of daily conduct. A mind controlled by knowledge, wisdom, and understanding produces a life worthy of the Lord. Although it seems impossible that anyone could walk worthy of the Lord, that is the teaching of Scripture. Paul desired the Thessalonians to "walk in a manner worthy of the God who calls you into His own kingdom and glory" (1 Thess. 2:12 NASB). He exhorted the Ephesians to "walk in a manner worthy of the calling with which you have been called" (Eph. 4:1 NASB). He told the Philippians to "conduct yourselves in a manner worthy of the gospel of Christ" (Phil. 1:27).[*]

---

[*] Adapted from "Colossians and Philemon," *MacArthur New Testament Commentary* (Chicago: Moody, 2007).

For Deeper Study (Optional)

Read Romans 5:12–21 below. Pay close attention to the italicized phrases.

On a sheet of paper or in your journal, note what these passages say (just the facts), what they mean (what can be implied from the text), and what they might mean to you. Once you have completed this for each passage, identify what you think the point is of Romans 5:12–21.

¹²Therefore, just as *sin entered the world* through one man, and death through sin, and in this way *death came to all men*, because all sinned—¹³for before the law was given, sin was in the world. But sin is not taken into account when there is no law.

¹⁴Nevertheless, *death reigned* from the time of Adam to the time of Moses, *even over those who did not sin* by breaking a command, as did Adam, who was a pattern of the one to come.

¹⁵But the gift is not like the trespass. *For if the many died by the trespass of the one man*, how much more did *God's grace and the gift that came by the grace of the one man, Jesus Christ, overflow to the many!*

¹⁶Again, the gift of God is not like the result of the one man's sin: *The judgment followed one sin and brought condemnation*, but *the gift followed many trespasses and brought justification.* ¹⁷For if, by the trespass of the one man, death reigned through that one man, how much more will those who receive God's abundant provision of grace and of the gift of righteousness reign in life through the one man, Jesus Christ.

¹⁸Consequently, just *as the result of one trespass was condemnation for all men, so also the result of one act of righteousness was justification that brings life for all men.*

¹⁹For just as through *the disobedience of the one man the many were made sinners*, so also *through the obedience of the one man the many will be made righteous.*

[20]The law was added so that the trespass might increase. But where sin increased, grace increased all the more, [21]so that, just as *sin reigned in death*, so also *grace might reign through righteousness* to bring eternal life through Jesus Christ our Lord.

Reflections

Hopefully last week you made a commitment to read, reflect, and meditate on the Word of God each day. Following are selections of Scripture provided as a starting point to drawing near to God through time with him. Read the daily verses and then record your thoughts, insights, or prayers in the space provided. On the sixth day, record a summary of what you have learned over the entire week through this study or use this space to write down how God has challenged you personally.

Day 1. If we claim to be without sin, we deceive ourselves and the truth is not in us. If we confess our sins, he is faithful and just and will forgive us our sins and purify us from all unrighteousness (1 John 1:8–9).

REFLECT

_____

_____

_____

_____

Day 2. He himself [Jesus] bore our sins in his body on the tree, so that we might die to sins and live for righteousness; by his wounds you have been healed (1 Peter 2:24).

REFLECT

_____

_____

_____

_____

Day 3. Clothe yourselves with the Lord Jesus Christ, and do not think about how to gratify the desires of the sinful nature (Rom. 13:14).

REFLECT

_____

_____

_____

_____

Day 4. For what the law was powerless to do in that it was weakened by the sinful nature, God did by sending his own Son in the likeness of sinful man to be a sin offering. And so he condemned sin in sinful man, in order that the righteous requirements of the law might be fully met in us, who do not live according to the sinful nature but according to the Spirit (Rom. 8:3–4).

REFLECT

_____

_____

_____

_____

Day 5. Since we live by the Spirit, let us keep in step with the Spirit (Gal. 5:25).

REFLECT

_____

_____

_____

_____

Day 6. Use this space to record insights, thoughts, or prayers that God has given you during *Session Two* and your *Reflections* time.

SUMMARY

_____

_____

_____

_____

THE NATURE OF THE FRUIT

MEMORY VERSE: Since we live by the Spirit, let us keep in step with the Spirit (Gal. 5:25).

Everybody Loves Raymond is a TV sitcom about a successful sports-writer named Ray Barone, whose oddball family made life interesting at its best, and complicated at its worst.

In one episode, for a gift, Raymond gives his parents a subscription to the "Fruit of the Month Club." The first month they get pears. Marie, Raymond's mom, asks him, "What are we supposed to do with all these pears?" When she finds out that she's getting more fruit the next month, and every month for a year, she practically panics: "Oh my goodness, what do I do with all this fruit?" Raymond says, "Most people . . . share it with their friends." Marie responds, "Which friends? . . . They buy their own fruit! Why did you do this to me?" She flails her arms and runs out of the room. "I can't talk, there's too much fruit in the house."

Marie was so overwhelmed with all the fruit in her house that she missed the point of the fruit—for healthy eating or to be given to others for their benefit.

We too might feel overwhelmed by the long list of "fruit" that God expects us to use and develop for the benefit of humanity. But as we will see in this session, the nature of the fruit is not overwhelming when we develop it, with the Holy Spirit's help, over time.

CONNECTING
10 min.

Begin your group discussion time by praying Psalm 86:11, which says: "Teach me your way, O LORD, and I will walk in your truth; give me an undivided heart, that I may fear your name."

1. Most people want to live a healthy, balanced life. A regular medical checkup is a good way to measure health and spot potential problems. In the same way, a spiritual checkup is vital to your spiritual well-being. The *Personal Health Assessment* was designed to give you a quick snapshot, or pulse, of your spiritual health.

   Take a few minutes alone to complete the *Personal Health Assessment*, found in the *Appendix*. After answering each question, tally your results. Then, pair up with your spiritual partner and briefly share one purpose that is going well and one that needs a little work. Then go to the *Personal Health Plan* and record one next step you plan to take in the area of the purpose you want to work on. If you haven't established your spiritual partnership yet, do it now. (Refer to the *Session Two Leader's Notes,* for the *Developing* section for help.)

2. Based on what you have learned so far in this study, share what you think "fruit that will last" (John 15:16) are.

GROWING
45–50 min.

We've been reflecting on the word picture "fruit of the Spirit" and all that it teaches us about the Christian life. In *Session One*, we saw that fruitfulness is God's purpose for us. In *Session Two*, we saw how it is the "flesh" that destroys our fruitfulness and we must fight the sins of the flesh. Now we will explore the nature of the Spirit's fruit that God produced in us to be lived out in our relationships with God and each other.

The Spirit's Fruit Is Produced by God

The fruit of the Spirit is not produced by us, but by God. It's the fruit of the Spirit, after all. We don't manufacture or produce our own fruit. God does.

3. What do you think is the believer's role in the production of the fruit in our lives?

The Spirit's Fruit Is Produced in Us

4. Galatians 5:22–23 says, "But the fruit of the Spirit is love, joy, peace, patience, kindness, goodness, faithfulness, gentleness and self-control. Against such things there is no law." What do these "fruit" represent in our lives?

5. How do you think that these "fruit" can be measured by our actions?

Read John 15:5–8.

6. Jesus is the vine tended by the Father. What do you think it means to not be fruit-bearing?

7. What happens to fruit when it is removed from its plant?

8. How does verse 5 help us understand the Spirit's work in our lives?

9. The idea of remaining in Christ is reiterated three times in this short passage. What is the implication of this?

The Purpose of the Spirit's Fruit

10. The fruit of the Spirit gives believers the power to fulfill their destiny in Christ. Look at the list in Galatians 5:22–23 one

more time. How are these qualities experienced and expressed in our lives?

Read 1 Peter 3:13–17.

11. The fruit of the Spirit are also used by God to draw people to himself through us. What does 1 Peter 3:13–17 say about how this might be carried out?

12. Can people in the world be drawn to God by his fruit in *your* life? Why or why not?

As we seek to understand the fruit of the Spirit, three vital insights and important reminders for us are: the Spirit's fruit is produced by God; the Spirit's fruit—its character—is produced in us; and the Spirit's fruit—its relationship principles—are used by God.

DEVELOPING 10 *min.*

Giving our hearts to God extends to loving his people. Galatians 5:13 says, "Serve one another in love." This is not optional. Our automobiles need all of their parts to run smoothly, and so does the body of Christ. God designed each of us uniquely to fill specific needs within the church. The infinite needs of countless people and circumstances around us require that we use our unique gifts in service to God and others.

13. Discuss some of the ways that we can serve the body of Christ. Is there a particular area of service that God has put on your heart to serve either in this group or in your local church? If not, investigate the opportunities and pray about finding a ministry in which you can serve. As you take that first step, God will lead you to the ministry that expresses your passion.

14. On your *Personal Health Plan*, next to the "Develop" icon, answer the "WHERE are you serving?" question. If you are not currently serving, note one area where you will consider serving.

SHARING

10 *min.*

Everyone searches for significance and purpose in life. The prophet Jeremiah offers encouragement in Jeremiah 29:11. It says: "'For I know the plans I have for you,' declares the LORD, 'plans to prosper you and not to harm you, plans to give you hope and a future.'" We can claim this promise as God's children. Sadly, many miss the opportunity to know God and the hope he gives. As we share God's love with others, we can offer true significance and purpose to them by introducing them to the One who promises to give it.

15. In the last session you were asked to write some names in the *Circles of Life* diagram. Go back to the *Circles of Life* diagram to remind yourself of the various people you come into contact with on a regular basis. Have you followed up with those you identified who need to connect with other Christians? If not, when will you contact them?

16. If you have never invited Jesus to take control of your life, why not ask him now? If you are not clear about God's gift of eternal life for everyone who believes in Jesus and how to receive this gift, take a minute to pray and ask God to help you understand what he wants you to do about trusting in Jesus.

SURRENDERING

10 *min.*

James 5:16 says, "Confess your sins to each other and pray for each other so that you may be healed. The prayer of a righteous man is powerful and effective."

17. Take some time now to begin the *Circle of Prayer* exercise. This exercise allows for focused prayer over each person or couple in the group. Each person or couple will have an opportunity to share any pressing needs, concerns, or struggles requiring prayer, and the rest of the group will pray for these requests. More complete instructions for this can be found in the *Leader's Notes*.

For Deeper Study (Optional)

Read Hebrews 12:5–11 below. Pay close attention to the italicized phrases.

On a sheet of paper or in your journal, note what these passages say (just the facts), what they mean (what can be implied from the text), and what they might mean to you. Once you have completed this for each passage, identify what you think the point is of Hebrews 12:5–11.

⁵And you have forgotten that word of encouragement that addresses you as sons:

> "My son, do not make light of the Lord's discipline,
>   and do not lose heart when he rebukes you,
> ⁶because the Lord disciplines those he loves,
>   and he punishes everyone he accepts as a son."

⁷*Endure hardship as discipline*; God is treating you as sons. For what son is not disciplined by his father? ⁸If you are not disciplined (and everyone undergoes discipline), then you are illegitimate children and not true sons.

⁹Moreover, we have all had *human fathers* who *disciplined us and we respected them for it*. How much more should we submit to the Father of our spirits and live!

¹⁰Our fathers disciplined us for a little while as they thought best; but *God disciplines us for our good*, that we may share in his holiness.

¹¹No discipline seems pleasant at the time, but painful. Later on, however, it *produces a harvest of righteousness and peace* for those who have been trained by it."

Reflections

If you've been spending time each day connecting with God through his Word, congratulations! Some experts say that it takes 21 repetitions to develop a new habit. By the end of this week, you'll be well on your way to cultivating new spiritual habits that will encourage you in your walk with God. This week, continue to read the daily verses, giving prayerful consideration to what you learn about God, his Spirit, and his place in your life. Then, as before, record your thoughts, insights, or prayers in the space provided. On the sixth day, record a summary of what you have learned throughout the week.

Day 1. So then, my beloved, just as you have always obeyed, not as in my presence only, but now much more in my absence, work out your salvation with fear and trembling; for it is God who is at work in you, both to will and to work for His good pleasure (Phil. 2:12–13 NASB).

REFLECT

_____

_____

_____

_____

Day 2. For by the grace given me I say to every one of you: Do not think of yourself more highly than you ought, but rather think of yourself with sober judgment, in accordance with the measure of faith God has given you (Rom. 12:3).

REFLECT

_____

_____

_____

_____

Day 3. For we know that our old self was crucified with him so that the body of sin might be done away with, that we should no longer be slaves to sin—because anyone who has died has been freed from sin (Rom. 6:6–7).

REFLECT

_____

_____

_____

_____

Day 4. Likewise every good tree bears good fruit, but a bad tree bears bad fruit. A good tree cannot bear bad fruit, and a bad tree cannot bear good fruit. Every tree that does not bear good fruit is cut down and thrown into the fire (Matt. 7:17–19).

REFLECT

_____

_____

_____

_____

Day 5. Have nothing to do with the fruitless deeds of darkness, but rather expose them (Eph. 5:11).

REFLECT

_____

_____

_____

_____

Day 6. Record your weekly summary of what God has shown you in the space below.

SUMMARY

_____

_____

_____

_____

LOVE, JOY, AND PEACE

MEMORY VERSE: A new command I [Jesus] give you: Love one another. As I have loved you, so you must love one another. By this all men will know that you are my disciples, if you love one another (John 13:34–35).

For as long as he could remember, Tim wanted out—he couldn't wait to leave and make decisions for himself. His mother was a woman of faith who knew Jesus as her Lord and Savior, but her parenting style made their home feel like a prison. Every opportunity and decision was analyzed and discussed until there was nothing more to be said. Every "allowance," whether it was an outing, a school activity, a purchase, or just hanging out with friends, came with conditions.

Tim had no doubt that his mom loved him, but he didn't understand her need to analyze, discuss, and manipulate everything until "correct decisions" were made. Tim was a good, godly person—he loved the Lord and was a straight A student who never got into any trouble. Tim came to realize that his mother's love was a "tough love" from an imperfect human who makes mistakes.

Conversely, Jesus's parenting skills are not flawed. In fact, Jesus is the only one who's perfect; he is the best example we have for what it means to embody the fruit of the Spirit. In this session, we'll begin to look at the character qualities and virtues imbued in the "fruit." We will look to Jesus's life to see how each of the qualities look in real life.

CONNECTING

10 min.

Open your group with thanks to God for what he has taught you during the last few weeks of your study of the *Fruit of the Spirit*. Pray also that God would open the eyes of your hearts to see his truth today.

1. Take five minutes to check in with your spiritual partner or with another partner if yours is absent. Share with your partner how your time with God went this week. What is one thing you discovered? Or, what obstacles hindered you from following through? Turn to your *Personal Health Plan*. Make a note about your partner's progress and how you can pray for him or her.

2. Jesus is the perfect embodiment of the fruit of the Spirit. Share a recent time when you looked to Jesus to know how to behave in a situation. What was the situation and what did you do?

GROWING

45–50 min.

We've been exploring the power, depth, and meaning of the biblical word picture in Galatians 5:22–23, the fruit of the Spirit. Now we will begin to look at the character qualities and virtues imbued in the "fruit" best modeled by Jesus Christ. We should look to his life to see what each of the qualities looks like in real life. Today we look at love, joy, and peace.

Love

Read 1 John 4:7–8. "Beloved, let us love one another, for love is from God; and everyone who loves is born of God and knows God. The one who does not love does not know God, for God is love" (NASB).

3. Why do you think being born of God and knowing God connects to loving one another (v. 7)? (See *Study Notes*)

Read 1 Corinthians 13:4–7. "Love is patient, love is kind. It does not envy, it does not boast, it is not proud. It is not rude, it is not self-seeking, it is not easily angered, it keeps no record of wrongs. Love does not delight in evil but rejoices with the truth. It always protects, always trusts, always hopes, always perseveres."

4. First John 4:8 tells us that "God is love." The word for love used in this verse is the same word used in 1 Corinthians 13. How is this love defined in 1 Corinthians 13:4–7?

5. John 15:13 says, "Greater love has no one than this, that one lay down his life for his friends" (NASB). How did Jesus demonstrate his unconditional, unlimited love for us according to this verse?

How does Jesus's sacrifice serve as an example for us today?

Read Matthew 22:37–40. "Jesus replied: 'Love the Lord your God with all your heart and with all your soul and with all your mind.' This is the first and greatest commandment. And the second is like it: 'Love your neighbor as yourself.' All the Law and the Prophets hang on these two commandments."

6. Jesus did not mince words when he told us how we are to live in this world. What do you think it means that "all the Law and the Prophets hang on these two commandments"?

How can we live our lives today as Jesus commanded?

Joy

7. Read the description of "joy" in the *Study Notes*. How does this description help us to understand what it means to be joyful in the biblical sense?

Read John 15:9–11. "As the Father has loved me, so have I loved you. Now remain in my love. If you obey my commands, you will remain in my love, just as I have obeyed my Father's commands and remain in his love. I have told you this so that my joy may be in you and that your joy may be complete."

8. What is the source of joy according to John 15:9–11?

What do we need to do to experience the joy described in this verse?

Read Hebrews 12:2. "Let us fix our eyes on Jesus, the author and perfecter of our faith, who for the joy set before him endured the cross, scorning its shame, and sat down at the right hand of the throne of God."

9. Jesus rejoiced in the hardship of the cross for the joy God set before him. What, or who, is the joy set before Jesus?

How should we respond to the knowledge that Jesus rejoices for us when we come to him?

10. The apostle Paul, despite great hardship and suffering and even a string of imprisonments, was a man of joy. While in prison himself, he had the audacity to boldly invite believers everywhere in all places to "rejoice in the Lord always. I will say it again: Rejoice!" (Phil. 4:4). How do we, like Jesus and Paul, rejoice in our own hardships and sufferings?

Peace

We hear lots of talk in our world today about peace-keeping missions. Jesus's mission is not a peace-keeping mission; it is a peace-making mission.

Read Colossians 1:19–21. "For God was pleased to have all his fullness dwell in him, and through him to reconcile to himself all things, whether things on earth or things in heaven, by making peace through his blood, shed on the cross. Once you were alienated from God and were enemies in your minds because of your evil behavior."

11. What does Colossians 1:19–21 and the *Study Note* on "peace" imply about our true spiritual state apart from Christ?

Read John 14:25–27. "All this I have spoken while still with you. But the Counselor, the Holy Spirit, whom the Father will send in my name, will teach you all things and will remind you of everything I have said to you. Peace I leave with you; my peace I give you. I do not give to you as the world gives. Do not let your hearts be troubled and do not be afraid."

12. Peace, like joy, comes from an understanding and internalization of all that God has done, is doing, and will do for us. With this in mind, what should believers be led to do?

The fruit of the Spirit are character qualities, or virtues, that the Spirit places in our lives. As we have seen, each is a window into the character and work of Jesus. Understanding each one drives us deeper into the heart of God and the gospel.

DEVELOPING
10 min.

First Peter 4:10 says, "Each one should use whatever gift he has received to serve others, faithfully administering God's grace in its various forms." Last session we talked about using our God-given gifts to serve him in the body of Christ. Today we will spend some time exploring the gifts we are given.

13. The Bible lists the many spiritual gifts given to believers. Take five minutes and review the *Spiritual Gifts Inventory* in the *Appendix*. Discuss which of the listed gifts you believe you may have. If you are unsure, you can review the inventory with a trusted friend who knows you well. Chances are they have witnessed one or more of these gifts in your life.

   Once you have an idea about what your spiritual gifts may be, discuss how you may be able to use them in ministry. Plan to investigate the opportunities available to you in your church and get involved in serving the body of Christ. It's amazing to experience God using you to fill a specific need within his church.

14. Briefly discuss the future of your group. How many of you are willing to stay together as a group and work through another study? If you have time, turn to the *Small Group Agreement* and talk about any changes you would like to make as you move forward as a group.

SHARING

10 min.

One of the ways we can be peacemakers in this world is by sharing the good news with others and helping them to grow in their new relationship with Christ.

15. In *Session Two*, you identified people within your *Circles of Life* that needed connection to Christian community. Jesus's commission in Acts 1:8 included sharing him not only within our own circles of influence (our Jerusalem), but also in Judea and Samaria and the ends of the earth. Judea included the region in which Jerusalem was located. Today, this might include neighboring communities or cities. As a group, discuss the following possible actions you can take to share Jesus with your Judea in a tangible way.

   ☐ Collect new blankets and/or socks for the homeless. Bring them with you next week and have someone deliver them to a ministry serving the homeless.

☐ Bring nonperishable food items to the next group meeting and designate one person to donate them to a local food bank.

☐ As a group, pick a night to volunteer to serve meals at a mission or homeless shelter.

SURRENDERING   *10 min.*

First Peter 1:22 says, "Love one another deeply, from the heart." One way we love one another deeply is to pray focused prayer over each other's needs.

16. Last week you began praying for the specific needs of each person or couple in the group during the *Circle of Prayer* exercise. Take some time now to pray over those for whom the group hasn't yet prayed.

Study Notes

Love: The word *love* used here signifies the true and pure love of God to his dear Son (John 17:26), to his people (Gal. 6:10), and to a depraved humanity that is in rebellion against him (John 3:16; Rom. 5:8). The very nature of God can be defined as love (1 John 4:8, 16). God's love prompts our obedience to him (James 14:21). Love encompasses the mind, emotions, and will of people because it comes from God.

Joy: The word for *joy* here denotes joy, happiness, gladness. It can refer to feelings and can result from circumstances (John 16:21), but for believers it is continual because of our relationship with Christ. Other use in Scripture describes the joyful response of the Magi (Matt. 2:10), the joy in heaven when a sinner repents (Luke 15:7, 10), and the joy in redemption (Heb. 12:2).

Peace: *Peace* is a state of being that lacks nothing and has no fear of being troubled in its tranquility; it is euphoria coupled with security.*

For Deeper Study (Optional)

Read James 3:17–18 below. Pay close attention to the italicized phrases.

On a sheet of paper or in your journal, note what these passages say (just the facts), what they mean (what can be implied from the text), and what they might mean to you. Once you have completed this for each passage, identify what you think the point is of James 3:17–18.

> ¹⁷But the *wisdom* that comes from heaven is *first of all pure*; then *peace-loving, considerate, submissive, full of mercy and good fruit, impartial and sincere.*
>
> ¹⁸*Peacemakers who sow in peace raise a harvest of righteousness.*

Reflections

Second Timothy 3:16–17 reads, "All Scripture is God-breathed and is useful for teaching, rebuking, correcting and training in righteousness, so that the man of God may be thoroughly equipped for every good work." Allow God's Word to train you in righteousness as you read, reflect on and respond to the Scripture.

Day 1. And hope does not disappoint us, because God has poured out his love into our hearts by the Holy Spirit, whom he has given us (Rom. 5:5).

---

* Adapted from *Mounce's Complete Expository Dictionary of New and Old Testament Words* (Grand Rapids: Zondervan, 2006).

REFLECT

_____

_____

_____

_____

Day 2. Greater love has no one than this, that he lay down his life for his friends (John 15:13).

REFLECT

_____

_____

_____

_____

Day 3. You, my brothers, were called to be free. But do not use your freedom to indulge the sinful nature; rather, serve one another in love (Gal. 5:13).

REFLECT

_____

_____

_____

_____

Day 4. You have made known to me the path of life; you will fill me with joy in your presence, with eternal pleasures at your right hand (Ps. 16:11).

REFLECT

_____

_____

_____

_____

Day 5. Blessed are the peacemakers, for they will be called sons of God (Matt. 5:9).

REFLECT

_____

_____

_____

_____

Day 6. Record your weekly summary of what God has shown you in the space below.

SUMMARY

_____

_____

_____

_____

PATIENCE, KINDNESS, AND GOODNESS

MEMORY VERSE: I have been crucified with Christ and I no longer live, but Christ lives in me. The life I live in the body, I live by faith in the Son of God, who loved me and gave himself for me (Gal. 2:20).

His name was Adoniram Judson from Massachusetts, but they called him "Jesus Christ's man in Burma"! This was no compliment in a country whose people bowed to Buddha and whose government officials let him know when he arrived that he was not welcome. Yet Judson persevered, even under threat of death, and sadly, death did claim his wife and two of his children. Believed to be a threat by the Burmese government, Judson was thrown into prison, where he stayed for two years.

But none of this deterred Judson from his mission to translate the Bible into Burmese and make disciples of the Burmese people. Almost forty years later, he had succeeded in doing both.

Few of us have the patience or perseverance of Adoniram Judson. We have lost sight of our character, commitment, and determination to do what is right regardless of the cost—choosing instead to take the path of least resistance. Yet, the kindest thing a Christian can do for a nonbeliever is lead him to eternal salvation. This often takes patient perseverance to accomplish.

In this session, we'll see how Jesus's life exemplifies this and two other fruit of the Spirit—kindness and goodness.

CONNECTING

10 min.

Psalm 100:4 says, "Enter his gates with thanksgiving and his courts with praise; give thanks to him and praise his name." As you begin your time together, offer a prayer of thanksgiving for all that God has done so far in your small group. Ask him to open your heart to receive his message for you today.

1. Check in with your spiritual partner or with another partner if yours is absent. Talk about any challenges you are currently facing in reaching the goals you have set throughout this study. Tell your spiritual partner how he or she has helped you follow through with each step. Be sure to write down your partner's progress.

2. Think of a time when your patience—with someone or in a difficult situation—paid off in some way. Was the result positive or negative? Share what you learned from your experience.

GROWING

45–50 min.

In this session, we continue our exploration of the fruit of the Spirit identified in Galatians 5:22–23 by looking at patience, kindness, and goodness. God, by his Spirit, forms these virtues deep in us. This happens as we walk by the Spirit, living daily by faith in the Son of God who loved us and gave himself up for us (Gal. 2:20).

Patience
Read 2 Peter 3:9.

3. God is patient in keeping his promises to us. What is the purpose of his patience?

Read 1 Peter 2:21–24.

4. First Peter 2:21–24 tells us that Jesus provides an example that we "should follow in his steps" of longsuffering patience. How can we practice patience in the midst of our tribulations and trials according to this passage?

Read Ephesians 4:2–3.

5. What behaviors are identified in this verse that can help us be patient while going through trials or waiting in anticipation for something to happen?

Is there one that is key to success?

Read James 5:7–8.

6. What will be the reward for our patience?

Kindness

Read Titus 3:4–6.

7. After reading Titus 3:4–6 and the *Study Note* on "kindness," how would you define God's kindness through this verse and the *Study Note*?

Romans 11:22 says, "Consider therefore the kindness and sternness of God: sternness to those who fell, but kindness to you, provided that you continue in his kindness."

8. God will show sternness to those who "fall" but kindness to those that continue in his kindness. What do you think it means to continue in his kindness?

What does this say about how God extends his kindness to people?

Read Ephesians 2:6–7.

9. What is God's purpose in the gospel and our salvation according to this verse?

In the NASB, Micah 6:8 reads, "He has told you, O man, what is good; and what does the LORD require of you but to do justice, to love kindness, and to walk humbly with your God?"

10. How is your response to the kindness of God evident in your life?

Goodness

Read Psalm 34:8.

11. Because God is good, he is a refuge for those who seek him (Ps. 34:8). What do you think one can do to discover the goodness of the Lord?

Read Psalm 100.

12. What does Psalm 100 tell us about the goodness of God?

How does this encourage you to seek him more fully?

Read Luke 18:18–19.

13. What was Jesus trying to communicate to the ruler who questioned him in Luke 18:18–19?

Read Galatians 6:8–10.

14. Galatians 6:8–10 encourages us to "do good." Why is Paul encouraging us toward good actions in this verse (v. 9)?

We're commanded to practice patience, show kindness, and do good to others. But God, by his Spirit, must form these virtues in us. That happens when we walk by the Spirit, living every day by faith in the Son of God.

DEVELOPING

10 min.

During the previous four weeks, hopefully you've developed some new growth disciplines such as accountability, Scripture memorization, meditation on the Word of God, and daily time with God. Consider taking your commitment to know God better one step further this week.

15. If you've been spending time each day in personal focused prayer, doing *Reflections*, and/or meditating on God's Word, consider taking your commitment a step further this week by journaling. Read through *Journaling 101* found in the *Appendix*. Commit this week to spending a portion of your time with God journaling.

16. During *Session Two*, you should have discussed whether your group would like to have a potluck or social. Take a few minutes now to tie up any loose ends in your plan.

SHARING

10 min.

Jesus wanted his disciples to share his gospel not only with their local communities, but also the world. *You* can be involved in taking the gospel to *all* nations.

17. Next to the "Share" icon on your *Personal Health Plan*, answer the "WHEN are you shepherding another person in Christ?" question.

18. In previous sessions you were asked to identify people who need to be connected in Christian community. Return to the *Circles of Life* diagram. Outside each circle, write down one or two names of people you know who need to know Christ. Commit to praying for an opportunity to share Jesus with each

of them. You may invite them to attend an outreach event with you or you may feel led to share the good news with him or her over coffee. Share your commitment with your spiritual partner. Pray together for God's Holy Spirit to give you the words to speak with boldness.

SURRENDERING

10 min.

Philippians 4:6 tells us, "Do not be anxious about anything, but in everything, by prayer and petition, with thanksgiving, present your requests to God." Prayer represents a powerful act of surrender to the Lord as we put aside our pride and lay our burdens at his feet.

19. During the past two weeks, you've been praying for the specific needs of each person or couple in the group during the *Circle of Prayer* exercise. Take some time now to pray over those for whom the group hasn't yet prayed. As you did last week, allow each individual to share the specific needs or challenges they are facing. Ask for God's transforming power to bring change to their lives.

20. Turn to the *Personal Health Plan* and individually consider the "HOW are you surrendering your heart?" question. Look to the *Sample Personal Health Plan* for help. Share some of your thoughts with the group.

21. Spend a moment silently praying as David did in Psalm 139:23–24: "Search me, O God, and know my heart; test me and know my anxious thoughts. See if there is any offensive way in me, and lead me in the way everlasting." Once you feel you've entered into an attitude of worship, sing a worship song or read Psalm 139 aloud together.

Study Notes

Patience: Patience, or endurance, is at the foundation of feelings and passions. It is suggested to mean "long of feeling"—a delay of one's response—as in longsuffering. Patience is first of all a quality of God. He shows his patience to the unrepentant (2 Peter 3:9), to the unsaved (2 Peter 3:15) so that he delays punishment (Rom. 2:4); his is a patience that shows his mercy. This word is used of human patience as well (Acts 16:3). As an aspect of the fruit of the spirit (Gal. 5:22) it is used to show that the believer should be patient with everyone (Eph. 4:2; Col. 1:11; 3:12; 1 Thess. 5:14; Heb. 6:12).

Kindness: Kindness is a characteristic of God. This word occurs only in Paul's letters. It denotes the kindness and good favor that God shows to believers. Paul reminds those who think that they are beyond judgment that it is only God's kindness and patience that forestall his judgment (Rom. 2:4). As a result of receiving the kindness of God, believers are to clothe themselves with kindness (Col. 3:12), to such an extent that it characterizes them even in the midst of trials and persecution (2 Cor. 6:6). Believers are able to exhibit kindness because of the work of the Spirit in their lives, for kindness is one of the aspects of the fruit of the Spirit (Gal. 5:22). Because unbelievers are without the Spirit, Paul can say that no one among them manifests kindness (Rom. 3:12).

Goodness: Goodness begins with moral integrity, but it is more than that. It's possible to be morally upright, but not good. Goodness is doing the right thing before God and in relation to people. Like kindness, it has an active care component to it. This word occurs only in Paul's letters. See also Kindness.*

* Adapted from *Mounce's Complete Expository Dictionary.*

For Deeper Study (Optional)

Read Luke 6:32–38 below. Pay close attention to the italicized phrases.

On a sheet of paper or in your journal, note what these passages say (just the facts), what they mean (what can be implied from the text), and what they might mean to you. Once you have completed this for each passage, identify what you think the point is of Luke 6:32–38.

³²*If you love those who love you, what credit is that to you? Even "sinners" love those who love them.*

³³And *if you do good to those who are good to you*, what credit is that to you? *Even "sinners" do that.*

³⁴And *if you lend to those from whom you expect repayment*, what credit is that to you? *Even "sinners" lend to "sinners," expecting to be repaid* in full.

³⁵*But love your enemies*, do good to them, and lend to them *without expecting to get anything back*. Then *your reward will be great*, and you will be sons of the Most High, because he is kind to the ungrateful and wicked.

³⁶*Be merciful*, just as your Father is merciful.

³⁷*Do not judge*, and you will not be judged. *Do not condemn*, and you will not be condemned. *Forgive*, and you will be forgiven.

³⁸*Give*, and it will be given to you. A good measure, pressed down, shaken together and running over, will be poured into your lap. *For with the measure you use, it will be measured to you.*

Reflections

The Lord promised Joshua success and prosperity in Joshua 1:8 when he said, "Do not let this Book of the Law depart from your mouth; meditate on it day and night, so that you may be careful to do everything written in it. Then you will be prosperous and successful." We too can claim this promise for our lives as we commit to meditate on the Word of God each day. As in previous weeks, read and meditate on the daily verses and record any insights you gain in the space provided. Summarize what you have learned this week on Day 6.

Day 1. When God made his promise to Abraham, since there was no one greater for him to swear by, he swore by himself, saying, "I will surely bless you and give you many descendants." And so after waiting patiently, Abraham received what was promised (Heb. 6:13–15).

REFLECT

_____

_____

_____

_____

Day 2. All men will hate you because of me, but he who stands firm to the end will be saved (Matt. 10:22).

REFLECT

_____

_____

_____

_____

Day 3. But love your enemies, do good to them, and lend to them without expecting to get anything back. Then your reward will be great, and you will be sons of the Most High, because he is kind to the ungrateful and wicked (Luke 6:35).

REFLECT

_____

_____

_____

_____

Day 4. But the wisdom from above is first of all pure. It is also peace loving, gentle at all times, and willing to yield to others. It is full of mercy and good deeds. It shows no favoritism and is always sincere (James 3:17 NLT).

REFLECT

_____

_____

_____

_____

Day 5. Therefore, as God's chosen people, holy and dearly loved, clothe yourselves with compassion, kindness, humility, gentleness and patience (Col. 3:12).

REFLECT

_____

_____

_____

_____

Day 6. Use the following space to write any thoughts God has put in your heart and mind during _Session Five_ and your _Reflections_ time this week.

SUMMARY

_____

_____

_____

_____

FAITHFULNESS, GENTLENESS, AND SELF-CONTROL

MEMORY VERSE: Whoever can be trusted with very little can also be trusted with much, and whoever is dishonest with very little will also be dishonest with much (Luke 16:10).

In May 2004, Sergio and his wife showed up at their Bible study meeting with some devastating news. Sergio had learned, that very day, that he had end-stage pancreatic cancer and had only three months to live. After the initial shock of the news, the group spent the rest of the meeting rallying around Sergio, crying and praying together.

Sergio accepted his fate with dignity and faithfulness to Jesus, who years earlier had saved him from himself and then restored his life to him. As the group prayed for him, Sergio became uneasy. One of the group members' prayer consisted of asking God for a miracle to heal Sergio. But Sergio would not hear it. He requested that if we were going to pray for him, he wanted it to be for God's will in his life, not our will.

For the next few months, the group provided as much physical and spiritual support to Sergio as possible. Sergio was resolute to serve God in this experience. He was ready to go home, if that was

God's will, but not before he shared with the world what Jesus had done for him. So only weeks before he went home to be with Jesus, Sergio went before the 15,000-plus attendees of his church to share his testimony with them.

Sergio's life was testimony to the power of the Spirit to produce fruit in our lives. In the midst of life's most difficult trial, even in the face of death, he demonstrated love, joy, peace, patience, kindness, goodness, faithfulness, gentleness, and self-control.

In this session, we'll look at the final three fruit—faithfulness, gentleness, and self-control—and how these manifest in our lives.

CONNECTING   *10 min.*

Begin this final session with prayer. Thank God for how he has challenged and encouraged you during this study.

1. This is the last time to connect with your spiritual partner in your small group. What has God been showing you through these sessions about his faithfulness? Have you gained a more full trust in his plan for your life? Check in with each other about the progress you have made in your spiritual growth during this study. Plan whether you will continue in your mentoring relationship outside your Bible study group.

2. Share with the group one thing you have learned during this study that has encouraged you. Also, if you have questions as a result of this study, discuss where you might find the answers.

GROWING   *45–50 min.*

We have been studying the fruit of the Spirit. We've seen six character qualities so far—love, joy, peace, patience, kindness, and goodness. In this final week of our study of the *Fruit of the Spirit*, we will inspect the final three fruit—faithfulness, gentleness, and self-control.

Faithfulness

The Scriptures tell us that God is faithful: "Because of the LORD's great love we are not consumed, for his compassions never fail. They are new every morning; great is [his] faithfulness" (Lam. 3:22–23). This is a great assurance when we experience temptation. He can be trusted.

Read 1 Corinthians 10:13.

3. What does God's faithfulness look like to believers according to this passage?

In the NLT, Hebrews 2:16–17 reads, "We also know that the Son did not come to help angels; he came to help the descendants of Abraham. Therefore, it was necessary for him to be made in every respect like us, his brothers and sisters, so that he could be our merciful and faithful High Priest before God. Then he could offer a sacrifice that would take away the sins of the people."

4. Jesus is called the merciful and faithful "High Priest" in Hebrews 2:17. How does Jesus's role as High Priest demonstrate his faithfulness to us (see the *Study Notes* for a definition of the "High Priest")?

5. How does God's faithfulness to us help us build and maintain faithfulness to him?

In the CEV, Daniel 6:13, 16–22 reads, "The men then told the king, 'That Jew named Daniel, who was brought here as a captive, refuses to obey you or the law that you ordered to be written. And he still prays to his god three times a day.' . . . So Darius ordered Daniel to be brought out and thrown into a pit of lions. But he said to Daniel, 'You have been faithful to your God, and I pray that he will rescue you.' A stone was rolled over the pit, and it was sealed. Then Darius and his officials stamped the seal to show that no one should let Daniel out. All night long the king could not sleep. He did not eat anything, and he would not let anyone come in to entertain him. At daybreak the king got up and ran to the pit. He was anxious and shouted, 'Daniel, you were faithful and served your God. Was he able to save you from the lions?' Daniel answered, 'Your Majesty, I hope you live forever! My God knew that I was innocent, and he sent an angel to keep the lions from eating me. Your Majesty, I have never done anything to hurt you.'"

6. Daniel was faithful to God, even to the threat of death in a den of lions. How does Daniel's display of faithfulness mirror the faithfulness you see in the lives of the Christians you know?

Gentleness

Read Matthew 11:28–30.

7. Jesus invites us to come to him and learn from him, for he is gentle and humble in heart. How does this verse reveal Jesus's gentle and humble nature?

What does it mean to take his yoke upon us? See the *Study Note* on the "yoke" for insight.

Read Colossians 3:12.

8. Just as Jesus shows his gentle and humble heart to us as he reaches out to relieve our burdens, we have a similar responsibility to the people around us. What should be our character according to Colossians 3:12?

Read Galatians 6:1.

9. What does Galatians 6:1 say our behavior toward others as Christians should be?

Read 1 Peter 3:15.

10. When we make our lives a witness for Christ, it should be with gentleness and respect. What characters of a gentle and respectful life are evident in a person's witness?

Self-control

Jesus was self-controlled. Never out of control, he acted appropriately in every situation and with every person. He resisted the temptations of the devil to turn stones to bread to demonstrate his power. With unlimited power and resources available to him at all times, he chose not to access or exercise them, but took the insults, the beatings, and the torture of those who eventually killed him. His crucifixion is the ultimate demonstration of Jesus's self-control.

Read 1 Corinthians 9:25–27.

11. Why should we discipline and control ourselves, our bodies, and our desires, according to this passage?

12. Based on our study of the fruit of the Spirit so far, what do you think is the "prize" mentioned in 1 Corinthians 9:27?

Read 1 Thessalonians 4:1–12.

13. God's will for us, according to 1 Thessalonians 4:1–12, is that we know how to live in sanctification and honor because we know God. What are the goals (v. 1) and benefits of living as described in this passage?

14. How does your daily living stack up against the requirements of 1 Thessalonians 4:1–12?

In a world that is filled with unfaithfulness, God calls us to faithfulness. In a world that is harsh, God calls us to gentleness. In a world that is out of control, God calls us to self-control.

DEVELOPING   *10 min.*

The *fruit of the Spirit* describes the qualities needed to live life in the Spirit. Everyone who puts them into practice can build toward a life of character like that of Jesus Christ. Christ is the model of perfect character. We can't achieve it all at once—we must grow toward it.

15. Prayerfully consider the following actions as a first step toward fulfilling Jesus's commission in your life.

☐ Hang a world map in the place where you pray at home. Pray for the world, then each continent, and then each country as the Lord leads you; or pray for the countries printed on your clothing labels as you get dressed every day.

☐ Send financial support to a missionary in a foreign country or a world mission organization. Your church will likely have suggestions for who this might be.

☐ Sponsor a child through a Christ-centered humanitarian aid organization.

16. If your group still needs to make decisions about continuing to meet after this session, have that discussion now. Talk about what you will study, who will lead, and where and when you will meet.

Review your *Small Group Agreement* and evaluate how well you achieved your goals. Discuss any changes you want to make as you move forward. As your group starts a new study, this is a great time to take on a new role or change roles of service in your group. What new role will you take on? If you are uncertain, maybe your group members have some ideas for you. Remember you aren't making a lifetime commitment to the new role; it will only be for a few weeks. Maybe someone would like to share a role with you if you don't feel ready to serve solo.

SHARING

10 *min.*

Scripture tells us that we should always be prepared to give the reason for the hope that we have found in Christ. That's what sharing Christ is all about.

17. During the course of this six-week study, you have made many commitments to share Jesus with the people in your life, either in inviting your believing friends to grow in Christian

community or by sharing the gospel in words or actions with unbelievers. Share with the group any highlights that you have experienced as you've stepped out in faith to share with others.

SURRENDERING   *10 min.*

Psalm 106:1 says: "Give thanks to the LORD, for he is good; his love endures forever." It is good to remember and give thanks for what the Lord has done.

18. Look back over the *Prayer and Praise Report.* Are there any answered prayers? Spend a few minutes sharing these in simple, one-sentence prayers of thanks to God. It's important to share your praises along with prayer requests so you can see where God is working in your lives.

19. Close by sharing and praying for your prayer requests. Thank God for what he's done in your group during this study.

Study Notes

Faithfulness: (belief, trust, confidence) The noun means "faith" in the sense of complete dependence and trust in God. It can mean faithfulness, as in one who maintains a life of faith.

High Priest: The High Priest refers to the highest religious office in Israel. The high priest was descended from Aaron, Israel's first high priest. His role was to officiate over the sacrificial ritual in the temple and to preside over the Sanhedrin. The most important duty of this priest was to enter the Most Holy Place on the Day of Atonement, one of the three most important days of the Jewish calendar (Lev. 16). On this day, after having made atonement for himself, he went behind the veil and made atonement for all Israel. He alone was able to stand in the presence of God. Hebrews describes Jesus as the ultimate and final high priest (Heb. 7–8) as well as the ultimate and final sacrifice, who accomplished "eternal redemption."

Gentleness: Gentleness is another notable characteristic of Jesus (2 Cor. 10:1). Twice in Matthew Jesus is called "gentle" (using the corresponding adjective) (Matt. 11:29; 21:5). Gentleness means to approach others (including one's enemies) in a humble and caring spirit, not using force to get one's way. Gentleness is something that should characterize Christians (Eph. 4:2; Col. 3:12; 1 Pet. 3:15). It is included as one of the nine aspects of the fruit of the Spirit in our lives (Gal. 5:23) and is part of how wisdom from above goes to work in our lives (James 3:13).*

Yoke: In Scripture, the word is used metaphorically to designate a burden, obligation, or slavery. The law as observed by the Pharisees was considered a heavy burden. The term in its literal meaning refers to a heavy wooden frame used to tie two draft animals together for pulling heavy loads such as plows and carts.

Self-control: The virtue of one who masters his desires and passions, especially his sensual appetites (Acts 24:25; 1 Cor. 9:25; Gal. 5:23; 2 Pet. 1:6, where it is named as one of the Christian graces). Occurs in Acts 24:25; Galatians 5:23; 2 Peter 1:6 (twice), in all of which it is rendered "temperance"; the RV marg., "self-control" is the preferable rendering, as "temperance" is now limited to one form of self-control; the various powers bestowed by God upon man are capable of abuse; the right use demands the controlling power of the will under the operation of the Spirit of God; in Acts 24:25 the word follows "righteousness," which represents God's claims, self-control being man's response thereto; in 2 Peter 1:6, it follows "knowledge," suggesting that what is learned requires to be put into practice.†

---

* "High priest" and "gentleness," adapted from *Mounce's Complete Expository Dictionary*.

† "Self-control," *Vine's Expository Dictionary of Old Testament and New Testament Words* (Nashville: Thomas Nelson, 1996).

Reflections

Get into harmony with God as you spend time with him this week. Read and reflect on the daily verses. Then record your thoughts, insights, or prayers in the *Reflect* sections that follow. On the sixth day record your summary of what God has taught you this week.

Day 1. The faithful love of the Lord never ends! His mercies never cease. Great is his faithfulness; his mercies begin afresh each morning. (Lam. 3:22–23 NLT)

REFLECT

_____

_____

_____

_____

Day 2. So if you are suffering in a manner that pleases God, keep on doing what is right, and trust your lives to the God who created you, for he will never fail you. (1 Pet. 4:19 NLT)

REFLECT

_____

_____

_____

_____

Day 3. Blessed are the gentle, for they shall inherit the earth. (Matt. 5:5 NASB)

REFLECT

_____

_____

_____

_____

Day 4. I press on toward the goal to win the prize for which God has called me heavenward in Christ Jesus. (Phil. 3:14)

REFLECT

_____

_____

_____

_____

Day 5. Now there is in store for me the crown of righteousness, which the Lord, the righteous Judge, will award to me on that day—and not only to me, but also to all who have longed for his appearing. (2 Tim. 4:8)

REFLECT

_____

_____

_____

_____

Day 6. Use the following space to write your prayer of commitment to continue spending time daily in God's Word and prayer.

SUMMARY

_____

_____

_____

_____

APPENDIX

FREQUENTLY ASKED QUESTIONS

What do we do on the first night of our group?
Like all fun things in life—have a party! A "get to know you" coffee, dinner, or dessert is a great way to launch a new study. You may want to review the *Small Group Agreement* and share the names of a few friends you can invite to join you. But most importantly, have fun before your study time begins.

Where do we find new members for our group?
This can be challenging, especially for new groups that have only a few people or for existing groups that lose a few people along the way. Pray with your group and then brainstorm a list of people from work, church, your neighborhood, your children's school, family, the gym, and so forth. Then have each group member invite several of the people on his or her list. Another strategy is to ask church leaders to announce that your group is open to new members.

No matter how you find members, it's vital that you stay on the lookout for new people to join your group. All groups tend to go through healthy attrition—the result of moves, releasing new leaders, ministry opportunities, and so forth—and if the group gets too small, it could be at risk of shutting down. If you and your group stay open, you'll be amazed at the people God sends your way. The next person just might become a friend for life. You never know!

How long will this group meet?
It's up to the group—once you come to the end of this study. Most groups meet weekly for at least their first six months, but every other week can work as well. We recommend that the group meet for the first six months on a weekly basis if possible. This allows for continuity, and if people miss a meeting, they aren't gone for a whole month.

At the end of this study, each group member may decide whether he or she wants to continue on for another study. Some groups launch relationships that last for years, and others are stepping-stones into another group experience. Either way, enjoy the journey.

What if this group is not working for me?

Personality conflicts, life stage differences, geographical distance, level of spiritual maturity, or any number of things can cause you to feel the group doesn't work for you. Relax. Pray for God's direction, and at the end of this study decide whether to continue with this group or find another. You don't buy the first car you look at or marry the first person you date, and the same goes with a group. Don't bail out before the study is finished—God might have something to teach you. Also, don't run from conflict or prejudge people before you have given them a chance. God is still working in you too!

Who is the leader?

Most groups have an official leader. But ideally, the group will mature and members will share the facilitation of meetings. Healthy groups share hosting and leading. This ensures that all members grow, give their unique contribution, and develop their gifts. This study guide and the Holy Spirit can keep things on track even when you share leadership. Christ has promised to be in your midst as you gather. Ultimately, God is your leader each step of the way.

How do we handle the child care needs in our group?

This can be a sensitive issue. We suggest that you empower the group to openly brainstorm solutions. Try one option that works for a while and then adjust over time. Our favorite approach is for adults to share the cost of a babysitter (or two) who can watch the kids in a different part of the house. In this way, parents don't have to be away from their young children all evening. A second option is to use one home for the kids and a second home (close by) for the adults. A third idea is to rotate the adults who provide a lesson or care for the children either in the same home or in another home nearby. This can be an incredible blessing for kids. Finally, the most common idea is to decide that you need to have a night to invest in your spiritual lives individually or as a couple, and make your own arrangements for child care. Whatever the decision, the best approach is to dialogue openly about both the problem and the solution.

SMALL GROUP CALENDAR

Planning and calendaring can help ensure the greatest participation at every meeting. At the end of each meeting, review this calendar. Be sure to include a regular rotation of host homes and leaders, and don't forget birthdays, socials, church events, holidays, and mission/ministry projects.

Date	Lesson	Dessert/Meal	Role

SMALL GROUP AGREEMENT

Our Purpose

To transform our spiritual lives by cultivating our spiritual health in a healthy small group community. In addition, we:

_____

_____

_____

Our Values

Group Attendance	To give priority to the group meeting. We will call or e-mail if we will be late or absent. (Completing the *Small Group Calendar* will minimize this issue.)
Safe Environment	To help create a safe place where people can be heard and feel loved. (Please, no quick answers, snap judgments, or simple fixes.)
Respect Differences	To be gentle and gracious to people with different spiritual maturity, personal opinions, temperaments, or imperfections. We are all works in progress.
Confidentiality	To keep anything that is shared strictly confidential and within the group, and avoid sharing improper information about those outside the group.
Encouragement for Growth	To be not just takers but givers of life. We want to spiritually multiply our lives by serving others with our God-given gifts.
Welcome for Newcomers	To keep an open chair and share Jesus's dream of finding a shepherd for every sheep.
Shared Ownership	To remember that every member is a minister and to ensure that each attender will share a small team role or responsibility over time. (See the *Team Roles*.)
Rotating Hosts/ Leaders and Homes	To encourage different people to host the group in their homes, and to rotate the responsibility of facilitating each meeting. (See the *Small Group Calendar*.)

Our Expectations

- Refreshments/mealtimes _____

- Child care _____

- When we will meet (day of week) _____

- Where we will meet (place) _____

- We will begin at (time) _____ and end at _____

- We will do our best to have some or all of us attend a worship service together. Our primary worship service time will be _____

- Date of this agreement _____

- Date we will review this agreement again _____

- Who (other than the leader) will review this agreement at the end of this study _____

TEAM ROLES

The Bible makes clear that every member, not just the small group leader, is a minister in the body of Christ. In a healthy small group, every member takes on some small role or responsibility. It can be more fun and effective if you team up on these roles.

Review the team roles and responsibilities below, and have each member volunteer for a role or participate on a team. If someone doesn't know where to serve or is holding back, as a group, suggest a team or role. It's best to have one or two people on each team so you have each of the five purposes covered. Serving in even a small capacity will not only help your leader but also will make the group more fun for everyone. Don't hold back. Join a team!

The opportunities below are broken down by the five purposes and then by a *crawl* (beginning), *walk* (intermediate), or *run* (advanced) role. Try to cover at least the crawl and walk roles, and select a role that matches your group, your gifts, and your maturity.

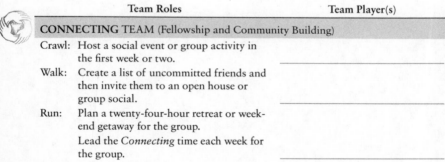

	Team Roles	Team Player(s)
	CONNECTING TEAM (Fellowship and Community Building)	
Crawl:	Host a social event or group activity in the first week or two.	
Walk:	Create a list of uncommitted friends and then invite them to an open house or group social.	
Run:	Plan a twenty-four-hour retreat or weekend getaway for the group.	
	Lead the *Connecting* time each week for the group.	
	GROWING TEAM (Discipleship and Spiritual Growth)	
Crawl:	Coordinate the spiritual partners for the group.	
	Facilitate a three- or four-person discussion circle during the Bible study portion of your meeting.	
	Coordinate the discussion circles.	

Team Roles	Team Player(s)
Walk: Tabulate the *Personal Health Assessment* and *Personal Health Plans* in a summary to let people know how you're doing as a group.	
Encourage personal devotions through group discussions and pairing up with spiritual (accountability) partners.	_____
Run: Take the group on a prayer walk, or plan a day of solitude, fasting, or personal retreat.	_____

SERVING TEAM (Discovering Your God-Given Design for Ministry)

Crawl: Ensure that every member finds a group role or team he or she enjoys.	_____
Walk: Have every member take a gift test and determine your group's gifts.	
Plan a ministry project together.	_____
Run: Help each member decide on a way to use his or her unique gifts somewhere in the church.	_____

SHARING TEAM (Sharing and Evangelism)

Crawl: Coordinate the group's *Prayer and Praise Report* of friends and family who don't know Christ.	_____
Walk: Search for group mission opportunities and plan a cross-cultural group activity.	_____
Run: Take a small group "vacation" to host a six-week group in your neighborhood or office. Then come back together with your current group.	_____

SURRENDERING TEAM (Surrendering Your Heart to Worship)

Crawl: Maintain the group's *Pray and Praise Report* or journal.	_____
Walk: Lead a brief time of worship each week (at the beginning or end of your meeting), either a cappella or using a song from the DVD or a worship CD.	_____
Run: Plan a unique time of worship through Communion, foot washing, night of prayer, or nature walking.	_____

PERSONAL HEALTH PLAN

This worksheet could become your single most important feature in this study. On it you can record your personal priorities before the Father. It will help you live a healthy spiritual life, balancing all five of God's purposes.

You will develop your *Personal Health Plan* as you move through the study material in this study guide. At appropriate places during the study, you will be instructed to identify your progress in one or more of the purpose areas (connect, grow, develop, share, surrender) by answering the question associated with the purpose. You may be instructed to discuss with your spiritual partner your progress on one or more steps, and record your progress and the progress of your spiritual partner on the *Progress Report*.

PURPOSE	PLAN
CONNECT	WHO are you connecting with spiritually? **Bill and I will meet weekly by e-mail or phone.**
GROW	WHAT is your next step for growth? **Regular devotions or journaling my prayers 2x/week.**
DEVELOP	WHERE are you serving? **Serving in Children's Ministry Go through Gifts Class**
SHARE	WHEN are you shepherding another in Christ? **Shepherding Bill at lunch Hosting a starter group in the fall**
SURRENDER	HOW are you surrendering your heart to God? **Help with our teenager New job situation**

PURPOSE	PLANNING QUESTION
CONNECT	WHO are you connecting with spiritually?
GROW	WHAT is your next step for growth?
DEVELOP	WHERE are you serving?
SHARE	WHEN are you shepherding another in Christ?
SURRENDER	HOW are you surrendering your heart to God?

DATE	MY PROGRESS	PARTNER'S PROGRESS
3/5	Talked during our group	Figured out our goals together
3/12	Missed our time together	Missed our time together
3/26	Met for coffee and review of my goals	Met for coffee
4/10	E-mailed prayer requests	Praying for partner and group
5/5	Great start on personal journaling	Read Mark 1–6 in one sitting!
5/12	Traveled and not doing well this week	Journaled about Christ as healer
5/26	Back on track	Busy and distracted; asked for prayer
6/1	Need to call Children's Pastor	Scared to lead worship
6/26	Group did a serving project together	Agreed to lead group worship
6/30	Regularly rotating leadership	Led group worship–great job!
7/5	Called Jim to see if he's open to joining our group	Wanted to invite somebody, but didn't
7/12	Preparing to start a group in fall	
7/30	Group prayed for me	Told friend something I'm learning about Christ
8/5	Overwhelmed but encouraged	Absent from group today
8/15	Felt heard and more settled	Issue with wife
8/30	Read book on teens	Glad he took on his fear
9/5	Talked during our group	Figured out our goals together
9/12	Missed our time together	Missed our time together

Progress Report

DATE	MY PROGRESS	PARTNER'S PROGRESS

PERSONAL HEALTH ASSESSMENT

Just Beginning	Getting Going	Well Developed

CONNECTING with God's Family

I am deepening my understanding of and friendship with God in community with others.   1 2 3 4 5

I am growing in my ability both to share and to show my love to others.   1 2 3 4 5

I am willing to share my real needs for prayer and support from others.   1 2 3 4 5

I am resolving conflict constructively and am willing to forgive others.   1 2 3 4 5

CONNECTING Total _____

GROWING to Be Like Christ

I have a growing relationship with God through regular time in the Bible and in prayer (spiritual habits).   1 2 3 4 5

I am experiencing more of the characteristics of Jesus Christ (love, patience, gentleness, courage, self-control, etc.) in my life.   1 2 3 4 5

I am avoiding addictive behaviors (food, television, busyness, and the like) to meet my needs.   1 2 3 4 5

I am spending time with a Christian friend (spiritual partner) who celebrates and challenges my spiritual growth.   1 2 3 4 5

GROWING Total _____

DEVELOPING Your Gifts to Serve Others

I have discovered and am further developing my unique God-given design.   1 2 3 4 5

I am regularly praying for God to show me opportunities to serve him and others.   1 2 3 4 5

I am serving in a regular (once a month or more) ministry in the church or community.   1 2 3 4 5

I am a team player in my small group by sharing some group role or responsibility.   1 2 3 4 5

DEVELOPING Total _____

SHARING Your Life Mission Every Day

I am cultivating relationships with non-Christians and praying for God to give me natural opportunities to share his love.   1 2 3 4 5

	Just Beginning	Getting Going	Well Developed
I am praying and learning about where God can use me and our group cross-culturally for missions.		1 2 3 4 5	
I am investing my time in another person or group who needs to know Christ.		1 2 3 4 5	
I am regularly inviting unchurched or unconnected friends to my church or small group.		1 2 3 4 5	

SHARING Total _____

SURRENDERING Your Life for God's Pleasure

I am experiencing more of the presence and power of God in my everyday life.	1 2 3 4 5	
I am faithfully attending services and my small group to worship God.	1 2 3 4 5	
I am seeking to please God by surrendering every area of my life (health, decisions, finances, relationships, future, etc.) to him.	1 2 3 4 5	
I am accepting the things I cannot change and becoming increasingly grateful for the life I've been given.	1 2 3 4 5	

SURRENDERING Total _____

	Connecting	Growing	Serving	Sharing	Surrendering	
20						Well Developed
16						Very Good
12						Getting Going
8						Fair
4						Just Beginning

○ Beginning Assessment   Total _____
☐ Ending Assessment   Total _____

SPIRITUAL GIFTS INVENTORY

A spiritual gift is given to each of us as a means of helping the entire church.

1 Corinthians 12:7 NLT

A spiritual gift is a special ability, given by the Holy Spirit to every believer at their conversion. Although spiritual gifts are given when the Holy Spirit enters new believers, their use and purpose need to be understood and developed as we grow spiritually. A spiritual gift is much like a muscle; the more you use it, the stronger it becomes.

A Few Truths about Spiritual Gifts

1. Only believers have spiritual gifts. 1 Corinthians 2:14
2. You can't earn or work for a spiritual gift. Ephesians 4:7
3. The Holy Spirit decides what gifts I get. 1 Corinthians 12:11
4. I am to develop the gifts God gives me. Romans 11:29; 2 Timothy 1:6
5. It's a sin to waste the gifts God gave me. 1 Corinthians 4:1–2; Matthew 25:14–30
6. Using my gifts honors God and expands me. John 15:8

Gifts Inventory

God wants us to know what spiritual gift(s) he has given us. One person can have many gifts. The goal is to find the areas in which the Holy Spirit seems to have supernaturally empowered our service to others. These gifts are to be used to minister to others and build up the body of Christ.

There are four main lists of gifts found in the Bible in Romans 12:3–8; 1 Corinthians 12:1–11, 27–31; Ephesians 4:11–12; and 1 Peter 4:9–11. There are other passages that mention or illustrate gifts not included in these lists. As you read through this list, prayerfully consider whether the biblical definition describes you. Remember, you can have more than one gift, but everyone has at least one.

ADMINISTRATION (Organization)—1 Corinthians 12

This is the ability to recognize the gifts of others and recruit them to a ministry. It is the ability to organize and manage people, resources, and time for effective ministry.

APOSTLE—1 Corinthians 12

This is the ability to start new churches/ventures and oversee their development.

DISCERNMENT—1 Corinthians 12

This is the ability to distinguish between the spirit of truth and the spirit of error; to detect inconsistencies in another's life and confront in love.

ENCOURAGEMENT (Exhortation)—Romans 12

This is the ability to motivate God's people to apply and act on biblical principles, especially when they are discouraged or wavering in their faith. It is also the ability to bring out the best in others and challenge them to develop their potential.

EVANGELISM—Ephesians 4

This is the ability to communicate the gospel of Jesus Christ to unbelievers in a positive, nonthreatening way and to sense opportunities to share Christ and lead people to respond with faith.

FAITH—1 Corinthians 12

This is the ability to trust God for what cannot be seen and to act on God's promise, regardless of what the circumstances indicate. This includes a willingness to risk failure in pursuit of a God-given vision, expecting God to handle the obstacles.

GIVING—Romans 12

This is the ability to generously contribute material resources and/ or money beyond the 10 percent tithe so that the church may grow and be strengthened. It includes the ability to manage money so it may be given to support the ministry of others.

HOSPITALITY—1 Peter 4:9–10

This is the ability to make others, especially strangers, feel warmly welcomed, accepted, and comfortable in the church family and the ability to coordinate factors that promote fellowship.

LEADERSHIP—Romans 12

This is the ability to clarify and communicate the purpose and direction ("vision") of a ministry in a way that attracts others to get involved, including the ability to motivate others, by example, to work together in accomplishing a ministry goal.

MERCY—Romans 12

This is the ability to manifest practical, compassionate, cheerful love toward suffering members of the body of Christ.

PASTORING (Shepherding)—Ephesians 4

This is the ability to care for the spiritual needs of a group of believers and equip them for ministry. It is also the ability to nurture a small group in spiritual growth and assume responsibility for their welfare.

PREACHING—Romans 12

This is the ability to publicly communicate God's Word in an inspired way that convinces unbelievers and both challenges and comforts believers.

SERVICE—Romans 12

This is the ability to recognize unmet needs in the church family, and take the initiative to provide practical assistance quickly, cheerfully, and without a need for recognition.

TEACHING—Ephesians 4

This is the ability to educate God's people by clearly explaining and applying the Bible in a way that causes them to learn; it is the ability to equip and train other believers for ministry.

WISDOM—1 Corinthians 12

This is the ability to understand God's perspective on life situations and share those insights in a simple, understandable way.

SERVING COMMUNION

Churches vary in their treatment of *Communion* (or *The Lord's Supper*). We offer one simple form by which a small group can share this experience together. You can adapt this as necessary, or omit it from your group altogether, depending on your church's beliefs.

Steps in Serving Communion

1. Open by sharing about God's love, forgiveness, grace, mercy, commitment, tenderheartedness, faithfulness, etc., out of your personal journey (connect with the stories of those in the room).
2. Read the passage: "And he took bread, gave thanks and broke it, and gave it to them, saying, 'This is my body given for you; do this in remembrance of me'" (Luke 22:19).
3. Pray and pass the bread around the circle.
4. When everyone has been served, remind them that this represents Jesus's broken body on their behalf. Simply state, "Jesus said, 'Do this in remembrance of me' (Luke 22:19). Let us eat together," and eat the bread as a group.
5. Then read the rest of the passage: "In the same way, after the supper he took the cup, saying, 'This cup is the new covenant in my blood, which is poured out for you'" (Luke 22:20).
6. Pray and serve the cups, either by passing a small tray, serving them individually, or having members pick up a cup from the table.
7. When everyone has been served, remind them the juice represents Christ's blood shed for them, then simply state, "Take and drink in remembrance of him. Let us drink together."
8. Finish by singing a simple song, listening to a praise song, or having a time of prayer in thanks to God.

Communion passages: Matthew 26:26–29; Mark 14:22–25; Luke 22:14–20; 1 Corinthians 10:16–21; 11:17–34

PERFORMING A FOOTWASHING

Scripture: John 13:1–17. Jesus makes it quite clear to his disciples that his position as the Father's Son includes being a servant rather than being one of power and glory only.

The Purpose of Footwashing

To properly understand the scene and the intention of Jesus, we must realize that the washing of feet was the duty of slaves and indeed of non-Jewish rather than Jewish slaves. Jesus placed himself in the position of a servant. He displayed to the disciples self-sacrifice and love. In view of his majesty, only the symbolic position of a slave was adequate to open their eyes and keep them from lofty illusions. The point of footwashing, then, is to correct the attitude that Jesus discerned in the disciples. It constitutes the permanent basis for mutual service, service in your group and for the community around you, which is laid on all Christians.

When to Implement

There are three primary places we would recommend you insert a footwashing:

- during a break in the *Surrendering* section of your group
- during a break in the *Growing* section of your group
- at the closing of your group

A special time of prayer for each person as he or she gets his or her feet washed can be added to the footwashing time.

SURRENDERING AT THE CROSS

Surrendering everything to God is one of the most challenging aspects of following Jesus. It involves a relationship built on trust and faith. Each of us is in a different place on our spiritual journey. Some of us have known the Lord for many years, some are new in our faith, and some may still be checking God out. Regardless, we all have things that we still want control over—things we don't want to give to God because we don't know what he will do with them. These things are truly more important to us than God is—they have become our god.

We need to understand that God wants us to be completely devoted to him. If we truly love God with all our heart, soul, strength, and mind (Luke 10:27), we will be willing to give him everything.

Steps in Surrendering at the Cross

1. You will need some small pieces of paper and pens or pencils for people to write down the things they want to sacrifice/ surrender to God.
2. If you have a wooden cross, hammers, and nails, you can have the members nail their sacrifices to the cross. If you don't have a wooden cross, get creative. Think of another way to symbolically relinquish the sacrifices to God. You might use a fireplace to burn them in the fire as an offering to the Lord. The point is giving to the Lord whatever hinders your relationship with him.
3. Create an atmosphere conducive to quiet reflection and prayer. Whatever this quiet atmosphere looks like for your group, do the best you can to create a peaceful time to meet with God.
4. Once you are settled, prayerfully think about the points below. Let the words and thoughts draw you into a heart-to-heart connection with your Lord Jesus Christ.

   ☐ **Worship him.** Ask God to change your viewpoint so you can worship him through a surrendered spirit.

☐ **Humble yourself.** Surrender doesn't happen without humility. James 4:6–7 says, "'God opposes the proud but gives grace to the humble.' Submit yourselves, then, to God."

☐ **Surrender your mind, will, and emotions.** This is often the toughest part of surrendering. What do you sense God urging you to give him so you can have the kind of intimacy he desires with you? Our hearts yearn for this kind of connection with him; let go of the things that stand between you.

☐ **Write out your prayer.** Write out your prayer of sacrifice and surrender to the Lord. This may be an attitude, a fear, a person, a job, a possession—anything that God reveals is a hindrance to your relationship with him.

5. After writing out your sacrifice, take it to the cross and offer it to the Lord. Nail your sacrifice to the cross, or burn it as a sacrifice in the fire.

6. Close by singing, praying together, or taking communion. Make this time as short or as long as seems appropriate for your group.

Surrendering to God is life-changing and liberating. God desires that we be overcomers! First John 4:4 says, "You, dear children, are from God and have overcome . . . because the one who is in you is greater than the one who is in the world."

PRAYER AND PRAISE REPORT

Briefly share your prayer requests with the large group, making notations below. Then gather in small groups of two to four to pray for each other.

SESSION 1

Prayer Requests

_____

_____

_____

_____

_____

Praise Reports

_____

_____

_____

_____

_____

SESSION 2

Prayer Requests

_____

_____

_____

_____

_____

Praise Reports

_____

_____

_____

_____

_____

SESSION 3

Prayer Requests

_____

_____

_____

_____

_____

Praise Reports

_____

_____

_____

_____

_____

SESSION 4

Prayer Requests

_____

_____

_____

_____

_____

Praise Reports

_____

_____

_____

_____

_____

SESSION 5

Prayer Requests

_____

_____

_____

_____

_____

Praise Reports

_____

_____

_____

_____

_____

SESSION 6

Prayer Requests

_____

_____

_____

_____

_____

Praise Reports

_____

_____

_____

_____

_____

JOURNALING 101

Henri Nouwen says effective and lasting ministry *for* God grows out of a quiet place alone *with* God. This is why journaling is so important.

The greatest adventure of our lives is found in the daily pursuit of knowing, growing in, serving, sharing, and worshiping Christ forever. This is the essence of a purposeful life: to see all these biblical purposes fully formed and balanced in our lives. Only then are we "complete in Christ" (Col. 1:28 NASB).

David poured his heart out to God by writing psalms. The book of Psalms contains many of his honest conversations with God in written form, including expressions of every imaginable emotion on every aspect of his life. Like David, we encourage you to select a strategy to integrate God's Word and journaling into your devotional time. Use any of the following resources:

- Bible
- Bible reading plan
- Devotional
- Topical Bible study plan

Before and after you read a portion of God's Word, speak to God in honest reflection in the form of a written prayer. You may begin this time by simply finishing the sentence "Father, . . . ," "Yesterday, Lord, . . . ," or "Thank you, God, for . . ." Share with him where you are at the present moment; express your hurts, disappointments, frustrations, blessings, victories, and gratefulness. Whatever you do with your journal, make a plan that fits you, so you'll have a positive experience. Consider sharing highlights of your progress and experiences with some or all of your group members, especially your spiritual partner. You may find they want to join and even encourage you in this journey. Most of all, enjoy the ride and cultivate a more authentic, growing walk with God.

HOW TO HAVE A QUIET TIME

Every relationship takes time to develop. You have to spend time with someone to take a relationship deeper. It's no different with our relationship with the Lord. A quiet time is time alone with the Lord. Each day we need to set aside time with him for Bible reading and prayer. As Christians, our primary goal is to become "conformed to the likeness of [God's] Son" (Rom. 8:29). "But one who looks intently at the perfect law, the law of liberty, and abides by it, not having become a forgetful hearer but an effectual doer, this man will be blessed in what he does" (James 1:25 NASB).

Five reasons to have a quiet time with God are:

- We need nourishment from God's Word to grow.
- We need to draw close to God.
- The Word is our best defense against sin.
- We need to be corrected when we sin.
- We need encouragement and comfort.

Three elements of an effective quiet time:

- Bible reading
- Prayer time
- Journaling and Bible note-taking

Tips for a meaningful quiet time:

- Recognize that you were created to be in relationship with God and he desires to spend time with you.
- Set a consistent time each day to spend with Jesus. Early morning or evening, children's nap times, and lunch hours are typical

times. If your quiet time is scheduled, you are much more likely to keep it.

- Get free from distractions (family members, telephone, TV, e-mail, etc.). Try to eliminate all sounds such as music that might keep you from hearing from God.
- If you miss a quiet time, don't beat yourself up over it. Realize that you got distracted or chose not to have that time that day. Just begin again. The longer you wait, the harder it is to make it a regular habit.
- If your quiet time is dry, difficult, or monotonous, try something new. Consider changing your Bible version, changing your location, listening to the Bible on tape, or changing your routine of reading and praying. Enjoy your time with God.

Beginning your quiet time:

- Pick a quiet place that works for you to meet the Lord.
- Have your Bible, notebook, and pen with you.
- Start with prayer by asking God to
  o meet with you
  o prevent distractions
  o reveal his Word for you today
  o bring comfort and clarification for your life
- Read the passage of Scripture you have selected for the day.
- Write down some of your observations from your Bible reading by answering the following two questions:
  o What does the passage say generally (what is it teaching me)?
  o What does the passage say to me personally (what should I do specifically)?
- Record any insights, thoughts, fears, concerns, praises, or feelings you have from your time with God.
- Respond to God in prayer in the following ways:
  o Praise and thanksgiving—"I praise you, God, for . . ."
  o Repentance and confession—"I confess my sin of . . ."
  o Guidance—"Lord, lead me today by . . ."
  o Obedience—"I will obey you in . . ."

LEADING FOR THE FIRST TIME
LEADERSHIP 101

Sweaty palms are a healthy sign. The Bible says God is gracious to the humble. Remember who is in control; the time to worry is when you're *not* worried. Those who are soft in heart (and sweaty palmed) are those whom God is sure to speak through.

Seek support. Ask your leader, co-leader, or close friend to pray for you and prepare with you before the session. Walking through the study will help you anticipate potentially difficult questions and discussion topics.

Bring your uniqueness to the study. Lean into who you are and how God wants you to uniquely lead the study.

Prepare. Prepare. Prepare. Go through the session several times. If you are using the DVD, listen to the teaching segment and *Leader Lifter*. Consider writing in a journal or fasting for a day to prepare yourself for what God wants to do.

Don't wait until the last minute to prepare.

Ask for feedback so you can grow. Perhaps in an e-mail or on cards handed out at the study, have everyone write down three things you did well and one thing you could improve on. Don't get defensive, but show an openness to learn and grow.

Prayerfully consider launching a new group. This doesn't need to happen overnight, but God's heart is for this to happen over time. Not all Christians are called to be leaders or teachers, but we are all called to be "shepherds" of a few someday.

Share with your group what God is doing in your heart. God is searching for those whose hearts are fully his. Share your trials and victories. We promise that people will relate.

Prayerfully consider whom you would like to pass the baton to next week. It's only fair. God is ready for the next member of your group to go on the faith journey you just traveled. Make it fun, and expect God to do the rest.

LEADER'S NOTES
INTRODUCTION

Congratulations! You have responded to the call to help shepherd Jesus's flock. There are few other tasks in the family of God that surpass the contribution you will be making. We have provided you several ways to prepare for this role. Between the *Read Me First*, these *Leader's Notes*, and the *Watch This First* and *Leader Lifter* segments on the optional *Deepening Life Together: Fruit of the Spirit* Video Teaching DVD, you'll have all you need to do a great job of leading your group. Just don't forget, you are not alone. God knew that you would be asked to lead this group and he won't let you down. In Hebrews 13:5b God promises us, "Never will I leave you; never will I forsake you."

Your role as leader is to create a safe, warm environment for your group. As a leader, your most important job is to create an atmosphere where people are willing to talk honestly about what the topics discussed in this study have to do with them. Be available before people arrive so you can greet them at the door. People are naturally nervous at a new group, so a hug or handshake can help put them at ease. Before you start leading your group, a little preparation will give you confidence. Review the *Read Me First* at the front of your study guide so you'll understand the purpose of each section, enabling you to help your group understand it as well.

If you're new to leading a group, congratulations and thank you; this will be a life-changing experience for you also. We have provided these *Leader's Notes* to help new leaders begin well.

It's important in your first meeting to make sure group members understand that things shared personally and in prayer must remain confidential. Also, be careful not to dominate the group discussion, but facilitate it and encourage others to join in and share. And lastly, have fun.

Take a moment at the beginning of your first meeting to orient the group to one principle that undergirds this study: A healthy small group balances the purposes of the church. Most small groups emphasize Bible study, fellowship, and prayer. But God has called us to reach out to others as well. He wants us to do what Jesus teaches, not just learn about it.

Preparing for each meeting ahead of time. Take the time to review the session, the *Leader's Notes*, and the optional *Leader Lifter* for the session before each session. Also write down your answers to each question. Pay special attention to exercises that ask group members to *do* something. These exercises will help your group live out what the Bible teaches, not just talk about it. Be sure you understand how the exercises work, and bring any supplies you might need, such as paper or pens. Pray for your group members by name at least once between sessions and before each session. Use the *Prayer and Praise Report* so you will remember their prayer requests. Ask God to use your time together to touch the heart of every person. Expect God to give you the opportunity to talk with those he wants you to encourage or challenge in a special way.

Don't try to go it alone. Pray for God to help you. Ask other members of your group to help by taking on some small role. In the *Appendix* you'll find the *Team Roles* pages with some suggestions to get people involved. Leading is more rewarding if you give group members opportunities to help. Besides, helping group members discover their individual gifts for serving or even leading the group will bless all of you.

Consider asking a few people to come early to help set up, pray, and introduce newcomers to others. Even if everyone is new, they don't know that yet and may be shy when they arrive. You might give people roles like setting up name tags or handing out drinks. This could be a great way to spot a co-leader.

Subgrouping. If your group has more than seven people, break into discussion groups of three to four people for the *Growing* and *Surrendering* sections each week. People will connect more with the study and each other when they have more opportunity to participate. Smaller discussion circles encourage quieter people to talk more and tend to minimize the effects of more vocal or dominant members. Also, people who are unaccustomed to praying aloud will feel more comfortable praying within a smaller group of people. Share prayer requests in the larger group and then break into smaller groups to pray for each other. People are more willing to pray in small circles if they know that the whole group will hear all the prayer requests.

Memorizing Scripture. At the start of each session you will find a memory verse—a verse for the group to memorize each week. Encourage your group members to do this. Memorizing God's Word is both directed and celebrated throughout the Bible, either explicitly ("Your word I have hidden in my heart, that I might not sin against You" [Ps. 119:11 NKJV]), or implicitly, as in the example of our Lord ("He departed to the mountain to pray" [Mark 6:46 NKJV]).

Anyone who has memorized Scripture can confirm the amazing spiritual benefits that result from this practice. Don't miss out on the opportunity to encourage your group to grow in the knowledge of God's Word through Scripture memorization.

Reflections. We've provided opportunity for a personal time with God using the *Reflections* at the end of each session. Don't press seekers to do this, but just remind the group that every believer should have a plan for personal time with God.

Inviting new people. Cast the vision, as Jesus did, to be inclusive, not exclusive. Ask everyone to prayerfully think of people who would enjoy or benefit from a group like this—then invite them. The beginning of a new study is a great time to welcome a few people into your circle. Don't worry about ending up with too many people—you can always have one discussion circle in the living room and another in the dining room.

For Deeper Study (Optional). We have included a *For Deeper Study* section in most sessions. *For Deeper Study* provides additional passages for individual study on the topic of each session. If your group likes to do deeper Bible study, consider having members study the *For Deeper Study* passages for homework. Then, during the *Growing* portion of your meeting, you can share the high points of what you've learned.

Session One God's Purpose for You

Connecting

1. Allow each participant to introduce themselves to the group. Whether your group is new or ongoing, there may be new people in the group who don't yet have an established relationship with the group. New groups will need to invest more time building relationships with each other.

2. A very important item in this first session is the *Small Group Agreement*. An agreement helps clarify your group's priorities and cast new vision for what the group can become. You can find this in the *Appendix* of this study guide. We've found that groups that talk about these values up front and commit to an agreement benefit significantly. They work through conflicts long before people get to the point of frustration, so there's a lot less pain.

   Take some time to review this agreement before your meeting. Then during your meeting, read the agreement aloud to the entire group. If some people have concerns about a specific item or the agreement as a whole, be sensitive to their concerns. Explain that tens of thousands of groups use agreements like this one as a simple tool for building trust and group health over time.

   As part of this discussion, we recommend talking about shared ownership of the group. It's important that each member have a role. See *Team Roles*. This is a great tool to get this important practice launched in your group.

   Also, you will find a *Small Group Calendar* in the *Appendix* for use in planning your group meetings and roles. Take a look at the calendar prior to your first meeting and point it out to the group so that each person can note when and where the group will meet, who will bring snacks, any important upcoming events (birthdays, anniversaries), etc.

Growing

Have someone read Bible passages aloud. It's a good idea to ask ahead of time, because not everyone is comfortable reading aloud in public.

4. Humanity began in a garden planted by God for our sustenance and growth. We were intended to live in that paradise forever.

5. The fruit of the garden was intended for food to enable the growth and health of humanity. God included life-sustaining water and plant life to keep our air breathable.

6. Humankind was placed in a perfect setting and set up for a test of obedience. The description of the garden with its trees and river leads up to the command, "You are free to eat from any tree in the garden; but you must not eat from the tree of the knowledge of good and evil, for when you eat of it you will surely die" (vv. 16–17). From the very beginning of time, humankind was designed to do God's will.

7. Adam was placed in the Garden to work it—to take care of it. Whatever work Adam did was in service to God. Man's purpose, then, is to serve God.

8. A mind filled with knowledge of the will of God comes through spiritual wisdom and understanding. This spiritual wisdom and understanding produces in us a life worthy of the Lord. We bear fruit that glorifies the Father; we grow in the knowledge of God; we are continually being strengthened with all power; and finally, knowledge of God, his promises and purposes, gives us the strength we need to endure trials and suffering.

9. When we let God be the gardener, the fruit that grows from our lives is used by him for his purposes. God plants the Spirit in us when we receive Jesus as our Lord and Savior. The Spirit produces fruit in us according to God's purpose for us.

12. Humans were created with the capacity for spiritual growth as well as physical growth. Paul recognized our part in our spiritual growth while acknowledging that God is ultimately responsible for the success.

13. Paul calls the work of the Spirit in us the "fruit of the Spirit." The fruit of the Spirit is the fruit that the Spirit of God produces in believers. But what does that mean? What is the Spirit? The Spirit of Christ is given as a gift to every Christian when we turn from our sins and trust Jesus Christ as Savior and Lord.

14. To help us grow, God places his Spirit in us to change us and grow us and produce fruit through us. To be "in Christ" refers to our identification with him in his life, death, and resurrection. He becomes our mediator and replacement.

15. Our lives produce the fruit of the Spirit.

Developing

This section enables you to help the group see the importance of developing their abilities for service to God.

18. The intent of this question is to encourage group members to set aside some time to spend with God in prayer and his Word at home each day throughout the week. Read through this section and be prepared to help the group understand how important it is to fill our minds with the Word of God. If people already have a good Bible reading plan and commitment, that is great, but you may have people who struggle to stay in the Word daily. Sometimes beginning with a simple commitment to a short daily reading can start a habit that changes a life. The *Reflections* pages at the end of each session include verses that were either talked about in the session or support the teaching of the session. They are very short readings with a few lines to encourage people to write down their thoughts. Remind the group about these *Reflections* each week after the *Surrendering* section. Encourage the group to see the importance of making time to connect with God a priority in their life. Encourage everyone to commit to a next step in prayer, Bible reading, or meditation on the Word.

Sharing

Jesus wants all of his disciples to help outsiders connect with him, to know him personally. This section should provide an opportunity to go beyond Bible study to biblical living.

19. Encourage the group to observe their interactions during the coming week with the intention of using these observations next week in evaluating the people who God has placed in their lives that he might want them to share with or invite to small group.

Surrendering

God is most pleased by a heart that is fully his. Each session will provide group members a chance to surrender their hearts to God in prayer and worship. Group prayer requests and prayer time should be included every week.

21. Encourage group members to use the *Reflections* verses in their daily quiet time throughout the week. This will move them closer to God while reinforcing the lesson of this session through related Scripture.

22. As you move to a time of sharing prayer requests, be sure to remind the group of the importance of confidentiality and keeping what is shared in

the group within the group. Everyone must feel that the personal things they share will be kept confident if you are to have safety and bonding among group members.

For Deeper Study

We have included an optional *For Deeper Study* section in most sessions. *For Deeper Study* provides additional passages for individual study on the topic of each session. If your group likes to do deeper Bible study, consider having members study the *For Deeper Study* passages at home between meetings.

Session Two Attack of the Flesh

Growing

3. Walking by the Spirit means living continually by faith in Jesus, the Son of God who loved us and gave himself up for us. It means continually looking to Jesus and what he's accomplished for us. It means always leaning on Jesus, who has so clearly demonstrated his love for us; and when we are captivated by his love, we will be changed by his grace, and the flesh will lose its power and allure.

4. Many Bible translations use the term "flesh" in this passage when talking about the sinful nature all people possess. When we hear the word "flesh," most of us think of our bodies. But that's not what Galatians 5 means when it speaks of the sinful nature, or "flesh." According to Scripture, our bodies are not bad. Our flesh is that sinful, selfish part of us that seeks to build a life apart from God. The flesh sets its desires against the Spirit and vice versa. They are in opposition to each other.

5. We are new creations in Christ, but we can choose to live either in the realm of the old age (in Adam), apart from God, or in the realm of the new age (in Christ). Paul helps us understand the difference between our identification with Christ, as opposed to living in the power of the "flesh."

6. Some suggest to be "obvious" means that they are public and cannot be hidden, but a better conclusion is that they originate with the sinful nature and not with the new nature received at becoming a new creature in Christ and so are intrinsically known by all.

8. These are immorality, impurity, sensuality, drunkenness, carousing (NASB). Self-indulgence or hedonism is one way we live our lives apart from faith, independent of God, by ourselves for ourselves.

9. These are idolatry and sorcery, enmities, strife, jealousy, outbursts of anger, disputes, dissensions, factions, and envy (NASB). These are common among people who, in their pride, can't seem to get along.

10. We can live apart from the Spirit and faith in God either by being very, very bad, or by being self-righteousness and prideful and hypocritical! Both self-indulgence and self-righteousness are ways we can live by ourselves, for ourselves, apart from faith and independent of God. Both are ways the sinful nature (flesh) can show itself in our lives. We need to be aware of and watch out for both. The monster within at times tends toward self-indulgence and at other times tends toward self-righteousness. It's our flesh that inhibits, thwarts, and destroys fruitfulness.

11. Restraining the flesh through self-effort is not the biblical answer. How can we fight it? Putting on the Lord Jesus Christ, which represents the continuing spiritual growth we gain when we have become children of God through faith in him. As long as we are in our earthly bodies, we will have sin within us. But we do not have to yield to sin's power. Because we have the Spirit within us, we do not have to succumb to the sinful nature (flesh).

Developing

14. For many, spiritual partners will be a new idea. We highly encourage you to try pairs for this study. It's so hard to start a spiritual practice like prayer or consistent Bible reading with no support. A friend makes a huge difference. As leader, you may want to prayerfully decide who would be a good match with whom. Remind people that this partnership isn't forever; it's just for a few weeks. Be sure to have extra copies of the *Personal Health Plan* available at this meeting in case you need to have a group of three spiritual partners. It is a good idea for you to look over the *Personal Health Plan* before the meeting so you can help people understand how to use it.

Instruct your group members to enlist a spiritual partner by asking them to pair up with someone in the group (we suggest that men partner with men and women with women) and turn to the *Personal Health Plan*.

Ask the group to complete the instructions for the WHO and WHAT questions on the *Personal Health Plan*. Your group has now begun to address two of God's purposes for their lives!

You can see that the *Personal Health Plan* contains space to record the ups and downs and progress each week in the column labeled "My Progress." When partners check in each week, they can record their partner's progress in the goal he or she chose in the "Partner's Progress" column on this chart. In the *Appendix*, you'll find a *Sample Personal Health Plan* filled in as an example.

The WHERE, WHEN, and HOW questions on the *Personal Health Plan* will be addressed in future sessions of the study.

15. Encourage the group to plan a social or potluck outside of small group time. Socializing together provides the group an opportunity to build stronger relationships between individual members as well as allows time for celebrating what God is doing through this small group Bible study.

Sharing

16. A *Circles of Life* diagram is provided for you and the group to use to help you identify people who need a connection to Christian community. Encourage the group to commit to praying for God's guidance and an opportunity to reach out to each person in their *Circles of Life*.

   We encourage this outward focus for your group because groups that become too inwardly focused tend to become unhealthy over time. People naturally gravitate toward feeding themselves through Bible study, prayer, and social time, so it's usually up to the leader to push them to consider how this inward nourishment can overflow into outward concern for others. Never forget: Jesus came to seek and save the lost and to find a shepherd for every sheep.

   Talk to the group about the importance of inviting people; remind them that healthy small groups make a habit of inviting friends, neighbors, unconnected church members, co-workers, etc., to join their groups or join them at a weekend church service. When people get connected to a group of new friends, they often join the church.

   Some groups are happy with the people they already have in the group and they don't really want to grow larger. Some fear that newcomers will interrupt the intimacy that members have built over time. However, groups generally gain strength with the infusion of new people. It's like a river of living water flowing into a stagnant pond. Some groups remain permanently open, while others open periodically, such as at the beginning and end of a study. If your circle becomes too large for easy face-to-face conversations, you can simply form a second or third discussion circle in another room in your home.

Surrendering

18. Last week we talked briefly about incorporating *Reflections* into the group members' daily time with God. Some people don't yet have an established quiet time. With this in mind, engage a discussion within the group about the importance of making daily time with God a priority. Talk about potential obstacles and practical ideas for how to overcome them. Encourage group members to refer to *How to Have a Quiet Time* in the *Appendix*

for ideas. The *Reflections* verses could serve as a springboard for drawing near to God. So don't forget these are a valuable resource for your group.

19. Be sure to remind the group of the importance of confidentiality and keeping what is shared in the group within the group. Use the *Prayer and Praise Report* in the *Appendix* to record your prayer requests.

Session Three The Nature of the Fruit

Connecting

1. Encourage group members to take time to complete the *Personal Health Assessment* and pair up with their spiritual partner to discuss one thing that is going well and one thing that needs work. Participants should not be asked to share any aspect of this assessment in the large group if they don't want to.

Growing

3. Our role is to tend to the soil of our lives by walking by the Spirit—living our lives by faith in Jesus, the Son of God who loved us and gave himself up for us.

4. The fruit of the Spirit represents the virtues or character qualities of our lives.

5. It's much easier to define a set of rules or standards and then measure ourselves and others against those rules and standards than it is to measure virtue or character. The fruit are outward signs of an inward change in our lives. Although they do not appear overnight, they are the proof that we are God's work-in-progress.

7. It begins to die and must be consumed while it is still fresh in order to be useful. But ultimately the fruit spoils if left to itself. And the longer it sits, the more spoiled and useless it becomes. The point of the illustration is that when we are separated from Jesus, we begin to die immediately. Our death becomes more complete the longer we are separated from him.

8. The Spirit's work in our lives has less to do with what we do on the outside than it has to do with who we are on the inside. Who we are is reflected in what we do, but the Spirit works from the inside out. This can be difficult to see because character and virtue is much harder to measure and quantify than behavior and rule keeping. Character is more nuanced and can be more vague.

9. Like waiting for the fruit to develop and ripen on the tree, we must be patient for the growth of fruit that results in our lives. As we abide in Jesus consistently and patiently, we will bear much fruit.

10. Seven of the nine character qualities listed are relational—excepting joy and peace. All the rest are experienced and expressed and lived out in our relationships with one another. It's easy to be patient, good and kind, faithful and gentle and self-controlled on a desert island when no one is around. And it's really quite impossible to love if there's no one to love. Virtue and character are tested and shaped and demonstrated and expressed in relationships. This is a great reminder that we were made for community—for deep and difficult, real and often hard, relationships—this is where our character is forged, virtue is developed, and the Spirit works.

11. People are inherently drawn to what they perceive as good. With all the chaos surrounding us every day, people search for whatever hope they can find. When they look at us and see God's unshakable hope that brings peace to our lives, they want to know what we know. We need to be ever open to the curiosity of others as we encounter them so that we can be ready to share our hope, Jesus Christ, with them.

Developing

13. The group members should consider where they can take a next step toward getting involved in ministering to the body of Christ in your local church. Discuss some of the ministries that your church may offer to people looking to get involved, such as the children's ministry, ushering, or hospitality. Remind everyone that it sometimes takes time and trying several different ministries before finding the one that fits best.

14. Encourage group members to use the *Personal Health Plan* to jot down their next step to serving in ministry, with a plan for how and when they will begin.

Sharing

15. It is important to return to the *Circles of Life* and encourage the group to follow through on their commitments to invite people who need to know Christ more deeply through Christian community. When people are asked why they never go to church, they often say, "No one ever invited me." Remind the group that our responsibility is to invite people, but it is the Holy Spirit's responsibility to compel them to come.

16. Take time in this session to extend to your group a call to receive Christ. You can do this using the video segment on the DVD, if you have it, or using the information below.

116

If someone in your group is ready to receive Jesus as their Savior now, lead them through the following steps and prayer:

Express acceptance and belief that Jesus died on the cross for you (1 Cor. 15:2–4).

Receive his free gift of forgiveness for your sins (Rom. 3:22).

Begin to live the life God has planned for you and live like you are forgiven (Mark 1:15; Rom. 12:2).

Tell Christ that you want him to lead your life from now on (Rom. 10:9).

You can use the following prayer or pray your own prayer; your heart response toward God is what's important.

Lord, I believe that you sent Jesus to die in my place to pay the price for my sins so I can be forgiven and enter into a relationship with you forever. Forgive me for my sins. I want to live the remainder of my life as you want me to. Fill me with your Spirit to direct me. Amen.

If anyone is not ready to receive Christ at this time, let them know that this is also something they can do at home later if they like. The important thing is to be sure that everyone has had the opportunity to receive Christ personally or have their doubts addressed.

Surrendering

17. It is common for groups to spend most of their time together in the areas of study and fellowship. When this happens, the time for prayer can get squeezed into the remaining minutes of the group. Consider this exercise after your group has met for a few weeks and is ready to go deeper in prayer support.

    Essentially, the *Circle of Prayer* is taking time to spend focused prayer time on each person, or couple, in the group. We suggest you allow each person, or couple, to share for a couple of minutes the needs they are facing. Then have that person stand, sit, or kneel in the middle of the room. The rest of the small group can then join hands around him or her, or place their hands on his or her shoulders if they are comfortable doing that. Group members can then take turns praying for the specific needs shared and ask for God's transforming power to bring change to the situations at hand.

    Since the *Circle of Prayer* takes time, begin doing this exercise this week and continue over the next two sessions so the group doesn't feel pressured to "rush" through the exercise for the sake of time. This time of prayer will bring your group closer together and will remind each of you of God's active presence in your lives. Don't forget to record the individual requests on the *Prayer and Praise Report* to remind you to continue praying for each other between group meetings.

Session Four Love, Joy, and Peace

Growing

3. Love is a product of the Spirit. Love marks a person as being of God since "love is from God." Consequently, someone "who loves" (in the Christian sense) has been "born of God" and "knows God." Love stems from a spiritually reformed nature and fellowship with God, which results in "knowing him." The absence of love is evidence that a person "does not know God."

5. When Jesus died for us on the cross, he demonstrated God's unconditional, unlimited love for lost, blind, dead sinners like you and me. Will we be faced with making this same kind of sacrifice? Probably not! Yet we are expected to sacrifice daily to show Christ's unconditional and unlimited love to his world.

6. The greatest commandment, the sum of all other commandments, is to love God with all that we are—our heart, soul, mind, and strength. The second greatest commandment is to love our neighbor as ourselves. The entire Bible develops and emphasizes these two points. Our lives as Christians should reflect God's love in us and be expressed, or passed on to the people around us. Love is so much more than feelings—love is a commitment, love is selfless, love serves. The more we grasp God's love for us in Jesus, the more love will grow in our hearts.

7. Biblical joy is more than happiness. It's contentment and dependence on God independent of our circumstances, rooted in all that God has done for us in Jesus. In other words, joy is not centered on what's going on in our lives, but rather in what God has done, is doing, and has promised to do in our lives. Joy comes from knowing who we are and whose we are.

9. We are his joy, his pleasure, his treasure!

10. We can follow Jesus's and Paul's examples by trusting the Lord and recognizing he has a plan and a purpose even in the hard things of life. This is what God intends to grow in us by his Spirit—this unshakable, unspeakable joy in his sovereign grace and purpose.

11. Sin separates and alienates us from God. Colossians 1:21 describes our true spiritual state apart from Christ. It says we were "alienated, hostile in mind, engaged in evil deeds," but Christ makes possible peace between sinners and a holy God. We have peace with God through our Lord Jesus Christ.

12. The peace we have in Christ through the gospel should lead us to become people who promote peace in a world filled with wars, conflict, and enmity. Matthew 5:9 says, "Blessed are the peacemakers, for they will be called

sons of God." Peacemaking is a mark of our sonship! Peace is something we possess in Christ. Peace is something we experience in Christ. Peace is something we promote and work for because of and for Christ.

Developing

13. Point the group to the *Spiritual Gifts Inventory* in the *Appendix*. Read through the spiritual gifts and engage the group in discussion about which gifts they believe they have. Encourage group members to review these further on their own time during the coming week, giving prayerful consideration to each one. We will refer back to this again later in the study.

14. It's time to start thinking about what your group will do when you're finished with this study. Now is the time to ask how many people will be joining you so you can choose a study and have the books available when you meet for the final session of this study.

Sharing

15. This activity provides an opportunity for the group to share Jesus in a very practical way. Discuss this and choose one action step to take as a group. Be certain that everyone understands his or her role in this activity. It might be a good idea to call each person before the next meeting to remind people to bring to the next session what is required of them.

Designate one person to investigate where to donate items in your area. That person can also be responsible for dropping off the items.

Session Five Patience, Kindness, and Goodness

Growing

3. The purpose of God's patience according to 2 Peter 3:9 is to give time for the unrepentant to turn from their sins and trust his Savior Jesus.

4. Jesus shows us the way. He entrusts himself to him who judges righteously. This is the key to patience—entrusting our circumstances, our causes, and ourselves to God who judges righteously, trusting that he is sovereign and will work all things, even our suffering, for his good. In all this, we endeavor to remain sinless—not being deceitful or retaliatory, not lashing out.

5. Love is key. If we can veil all our actions with love, then humility, gentleness, peace, and patience become easier to attain.

6. Because God has been and is patient toward us, we his people are also called to patience while we wait for our reward—the Lord's coming.

7. Kindness is care in feeling and action, and is the extension of God's grace toward others. Jesus is the embodiment of God's kindness! The giving of Jesus and the Holy Spirit is an expression of God's kindness to us.

8. God is a just god; we cannot take his kindness for granted.

9. God has saved us so that he might forever show his everlasting kindness to us.

13. Jesus is challenging the ruler's conception of what "good" means. When the man calls Jesus "good teacher," he is using the term to mean "a good person; righteous." Jesus's response says, "You don't really understand what good is. True goodness is God's perfection, and no human being can achieve this." In other words, the man's conception of goodness (= earned righteousness) is wrong. It is faith in God alone that saves, not human goodness. This is the nature of true goodness.

14. The Lord is good toward us, and we are called to be and do good toward others—not to gain the favor of men, but to please the Spirit.

Developing

15. If members of the group have committed to spending time alone with God, congratulate them and encourage them to take their commitment one step further and begin journaling. Review *Journaling 101* in the *Appendix* prior to your group time so that you are familiar with what it contains.

Sharing

17. Encourage group members to think about when they are shepherding another person in Christ. This could be simply following through on inviting someone to church or reaching out to them in Christ's love. Then have everyone answer the question "WHEN are you shepherding another person in Christ?" on the *Personal Health Plan*.

18. It is important to return to the *Circles of Life* often, both to encourage the group to follow through on their commitments as well as to foster growth toward new commitments. Encourage the group this week to consider reaching out to their non-Christian friends, family, and acquaintances. Remind everyone that our responsibility is to share Jesus with others, but it is the Holy Spirit's responsibility to convict souls and bring forth change.

Surrendering

20. Have everyone answer the question "HOW are you surrendering your heart?" on the *Personal Health Plan.*

Session Six Faithfulness, Gentleness, and Self-control

Connecting

2. Take a few minutes for group members to share one thing they learned or a commitment they made or renewed during this study. They may also want to share what they enjoyed most about the study and about this group.

    Be prepared to offer some suggested resources for answering questions that may arise from this study. Offer other Scripture that relates to the topics studied. Ask your pastor to suggest some helpful books or articles. Advise group members to schedule a meeting with a pastor to get answers to difficult questions. Whatever you do, don't let anyone leave with unanswered questions or without the resources to find the answers they seek.

Growing

3. First Corinthians 10:13 tells us God's faithfulness is trustworthy—he is loyal, reliable, and dependable.

4. We see the faithfulness of God in the face of Christ who became man, and our "High Priest," so that he could pay the penalty for our sins through his sacrifice. Jesus was faithful in his obedience. He lived the life that God requires for us and then died in our place.

5. Our faithfulness builds over time as we consistently trust the Lord. Faith in God and his gospel makes us faithful people.

6. Daniel, steadfast in his faith and devotion, refused to compromise or bow to the idols of the worldly culture around him. Daniel was faithful even as he faced the lions' den. Faithfulness in the lives of Christians today shouldn't look much different than that. We too are called to be faithful like Daniel was.

7. Jesus shows his care and love for us by inviting the weary and burdened to find rest in him. The law was a "yoke" that was considered hard to bear. Jesus used this familiar phrasing as an invitation to discipleship. We will not be free from all constraints; we will still carry a yoke, but it will be light (v. 30).

8. The gospel is the reason for our gentleness and the way to gentleness and all other virtues. Because we've been chosen by God, set apart by God,

and loved by God, the gospel shows in all these things, we can put on gentleness.

9. When someone stumbles, they should be lifted up gently. We are to "restore such a one in a spirit of gentleness" (NASB) when they sin.

10. We are to be ready to give an answer for our hope in Christ to others who ask and yet to do it, not defensively or harshly, but with gentleness and reverence (1 Peter 3:15). Gentleness, in other words, is to shape the way we interact with all others.

12. We are living in a world that encourages us in every way to enjoy ourselves and indulge ourselves—not to control ourselves. This virtue, like so many others in the list, is not valued or encouraged in our world today. It's laughed at and scorned. Self-control is considered prudish and outdated. But 1 Corinthians 9 says that Christians should think like athletes; we discipline and control ourselves, our bodies, and our desires because we've got our eyes fixed on the imperishable victor's crown.

13. The ultimate goal is to "live in order to please God." The benefits are that each person would 1) learn to control his own body in a way that is holy and honorable, 2) live a holy life, 3) love each other, 4) live a daily life that wins the respect of outsiders, and 5) live such that you will not be dependent on anybody except God. All these things lead to self-control.

Developing

15. Discuss the implication of Jesus's mandate on the lives of believers today to take the gospel to the "ends of the earth." Have each person consider the action steps listed and choose one to begin immediately as a way of doing their part in seeing this accomplished.

16. If you haven't already done so, you'll want to take time to finalize plans for the future of your group. You need to talk about whether you will continue together as a group, who will lead, and where you will meet.

   As you discuss the future of your group, talk about how well you achieved the goals you made in the *Small Group Agreement*. Address any changes you'd like to make as you move forward.

Sharing

17. Allow one or two group members to share for a few minutes a testimony about how they helped someone connect in Christian community or shared Jesus with an unbelieving friend or relative.

Surrendering

18. Spend a few minutes devoted solely to sharing praises aloud in simple, one-sentence prayers. Be sure to allow time to share prayer requests. Have one person close the meeting with prayer.

19. Don't forget to close this group time in prayer, praising God for all he accomplished in and through everyone. You can refer back to your *Prayer and Praise Report* for specific praises.

SMALL GROUP ROSTER

Name	Address	Phone	E-mail Address	Team or Role	When/How to Contact You

Pass your book around your group at your first meeting to get everyone's name and contact information.

Name	Address	Phone	E-mail Address	Team or Role	When/How to Contact You

DEEPENING LIFE TOGETHER SERIES

Six **NEW** Studies Now Available!

FRUIT OF THE SPIRIT

JAMES

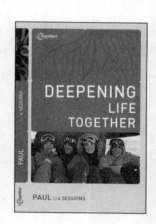

PAUL

PSALMS

RUTH

SERMON ON THE MOUNT

Deepening Life Together is an innovative approach to group Bible study in a DVD format built on the five biblical purposes: **connecting, growing, developing, sharing, and surrendering.**

Each session includes a traditional study guide and a DVD with insightful teaching from trusted scholars and pastors. Included on each DVD are pre-session training videos for leaders and footage from the bestselling *Jesus Film.*

Lifetogether has developed and sold over 2.5 million copies of bestselling, award-winning curriculum for small groups. This DVD series—perfect for small group ministries, Sunday school classes, and Bible study groups—will improve your worship, fellowship, discipleship, evangelism, and ministry.

Studies Available:

ACTS

PRAYING
GOD'S WAY

EPHESIANS

PROMISES
OF GOD

JOHN

PARABLES

REVELATION

ROMANS

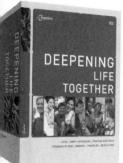

DEEPENING LIFE TOGETHER KIT

The kit includes 8 discussion guides and 8 DVDs: Acts, Romans, John, Ephesians, Revelation, Praying God's Way, Promises of God, and Parables

BakerBooks
a division of Baker Publishing Group
www.BakerBooks.com